P9-ELX-435

The Art
of
Flaneuring

The Art

of

Flaneuring

How to Wander with Intention
and Discover a Better Life

ERIKA OWEN

Tiller Press

NEW YORK   LONDON   TORONTO   SYDNEY   NEW DELHI

TILLER PRESS

An Imprint of Simon & Schuster, Inc.
1230 Avenue of the Americas
New York, NY 10020

Copyright © 2019 by Simon & Schuster, Inc.

Illustrations by Sarah Smith

All rights reserved, including the right to reproduce this book or portions
thereof in any form whatsoever. For information, address
Simon & Schuster Subsidiary Rights Department,
1230 Avenue of the Americas, New York, NY 10020.

First Tiller Press hardcover edition October 2019

TILLER PRESS and colophon are trademarks of Simon & Schuster, Inc.

For information about special discounts for bulk purchases,
please contact Simon & Schuster Special Sales at 1-866-506-1949
or business@simonandschuster.com.

The Simon & Schuster Speakers Bureau can bring authors to your
live event. For more information or to book an event, contact
the Simon & Schuster Speakers Bureau at 1-866-248-3049
or visit our website at www.simonspeakers.com.

Interior design by Paul Dippolito

Manufactured in the United States of America

1   3   5   7   9   10   8   6   4   2

Library of Congress Cataloging-in-Publication Data is available.

ISBN 978-1-9821-3351-1
ISBN 978-1-9821-3352-8 (ebook)

*To my ever-inspiring brother Ryan (the "Good One"),
who taught me that understanding how your body moves
is one of the greatest acts of self-care you can participate in.
This is also for all of the people who have seen me silently
stomp out of a room; I promise, it was for your own good.*

Contents

The Art
of
Flaneuring

Introduction

What on Earth Is Flaneuring?

You know those feelings that often have a German word associated with them—words that you have no chance of pronouncing correctly? Take *Fremdschämen*, for example. This word defines a feeling we all have experienced: a deep shame for someone else in an uncomfortable situation, one that doesn't exactly involve us. A stranger tripping and falling, spilling his entire coffee on the innocent bystander dressed in white in front of him. A server trying to explain to a vegetarian that her veggie burger is actually a real meat burger ... after she's already taken a bite. Your manager berating one of your coworkers about something that wasn't his fault. *Flâneur* isn't a German word—it's French—but it falls into the same bucket of expressions. It describes an action and a way of being that you may never have realized there was a word for.

In the nineteenth century, the word *flâneur* referred to a well-to-do, dandy type of white man—and usually a Parisian—who would idly stroll through the streets of a city, carefully observing his everyday surroundings and finding the beauty in what many would consider the mundane. The kind of strolling these early flaneurs did was always done with a romantic mind-set—or a greater focus on finding meaning in the cracks in the street than getting somewhere specific—and more often than not it was also done while slightly drunk.

But much like the beloved Danish concept of *hygge*, which emphasizes the value in being comfy and cozy, behaving like a flaneur—something the French originally called *flânerie* and many have since colloquially starting calling *flaneuring*, without the diacritic over the *a*—can also be a lifestyle. Over the years, and as more and more people have discovered flaneuring's many benefits, *to flaneur* has evolved to more generally mean "to wander with intention"—or, in other words, "to be intentionally aimless." Flaneuring, essentially, is taking a walk for the sake of taking a walk—not to stop by the bank, not to get some exercise, not to get directly from point A to point B. All these things can happen while you're flaneuring, but the objective of a flaneur is to enjoy the journey for what it is—to look outward and let what you see influence your inward thoughts, to be a part of the scenery while also taking a moment to deeply appreciate the environment that surrounds you.

Here are a few brief examples of ways you can easily incorporate some flaneuring into your everyday life:

Killing Time Before Meeting Friends for Dinner

We've all been there: arriving at a restaurant before our dining companions have shown up and needing a way to kill time. Instead of mindlessly scrolling through your phone (yet again), try taking a walk around the block. Read all of the storefront names as you walk by, making mental notes of ones that make you giggle, think, and scratch your head. If there isn't a block to walk around, find a spot to perch and people-watch. Count the cars that drive by. Read their license plates and try to make out meanings for their letters as acronyms.

Searching for the Perfect Picnic Spot

Pick a park or a beach and start walking. A picnic can be anything you want it to be: a random selection of snacks, a bit of bread and cheese, a single beer, a full-on tapas-inspired spread. There are no rules when it comes to picnic foods, and anyone who tells you differently is certainly not a friend, in my opinion!

Exploring a New Park

Parks are the perfect places to practice your flaneuring. Not only do the preset boundaries create a safe space for exploring, but there are often a lot of different scenes to take in: dog runs, playgrounds, ponds, forested areas, bike paths. If you're finding yourself fighting against the distraction of having a wide choice of scenery, focus on making a mental map of the park. The next time you visit, spend time acknowledging more of the details.

Window-Shopping While on a Trip

Window-shopping is another fantastic way to fla-neur, so the next time you're on a trip in a new location, head into a local store and take in the details. Are the signs and advertisements in English or the local dialect? That will tell you a lot about how many tourists an area sees. Are you seeing a local artist pop up more than the rest? What style of clothing or what kinds of items do you see being sold—and does it inspire you? Observe what all of the shopkeepers and employees are wearing. You can learn so much about a new place based on the items sold in its stores.

Taking a Walk to Calm Your Mind

If you're working through something tough or anxiety inducing, pulling yourself out of a familiar environment can often give you the kick you need to come up with a solution, or something close to one. In this instance, don't push yourself to calm down. Let your thoughts wander, and remember that your brain is still working hard on big problems even when you aren't consciously thinking about them, and it might just take some fresh air to clear out all of the noise.

Walking Your Dog

What better way to flaneur than letting an excited pup on a leash guide you on a walk? If you don't have a dog, chances are good that a friend who does have one will leap at the opportunity for a break as the designated walker.

As I hope to have shown in these examples, flaneuring is relatively simple, but to truly appreciate its many benefits it's worth learning about its origins as well as the many forms it can take. If flaneuring sounds like something you might like to do—and I'm assuming it is since you're reading this book—but getting started is a bit intimidating, take solace that you've likely already flaneured at some point in your life. I'd even go as far as saying that babies, with their nerve-racking crawling and tendency to get into things they probably shouldn't, are the ultimate early-life flaneurs. (Too bad most of us can't remember what discovering a stairwell for the first time felt like.)

Flaneuring can bring a lot of unexpected and beautiful moments into your day, and when you wander with intention, you'll find your brain can do some pretty great work. Not only is flaneuring a good way to clear those daily nagging thoughts out of your mind and replace them with more positive and productive ideas, it can also be a great way to get some fresh air. Everyone could always use more fresh air.

By reading this book, my hope is that you'll ultimately come to better understand how embracing your inner flaneur can help you experience the world in a new way, spark creativity you never knew was in that brain of yours, switch up your daily routines, more effectively deal with stress, and so much more.

Ready to begin? Let's get started.

A Brief History of the Flaneur

At the most basic, a flaneur is someone who strolls. But in the late nineteenth century, to be called a flaneur was a much more exclusive description. It often meant that you were a middle- or upper-class white man who had achieved a level within society with the privilege of living a life of leisure—or at least enough time in your day to walk without a care in the world—and a level that arguably made you an interesting and intellectual person to talk to at parties.

The French poet Charles Baudelaire was one of the first people to define a flaneur as such, by describing him in his essay "The Painter of Modern Life" as a "gentleman stroller of city streets," or one who casually but thoughtfully observed and experienced modern-day urban life as he walked. We all know now that men are not the only people capable of being flaneurs, but women during this time, namely middle- or upper-class white women, did not flaneur. The women who did flaneur were, perhaps unsurprisingly, not met with the same sort of romantic appreciation as male flaneurs. A woman who freely walked the streets in the nineteenth century, unaccompanied by a man, was placed in another section of society entirely, one far from valued or regarded with admiration. More often than not, these female flaneurs would be thought of as what we now call sex workers, which, as you can imagine, was not widely regarded as a respectable profession in nineteenth-century France. So, for the sake of defining the term at its time of conception, I'll leave it at this:

middle- and upper-class white men were the only socially acceptable flaneurs in France during that time.

Whereas Baudelaire introduced these male flaneurs into society in the nineteenth century, Christopher Butler, an author and professor of English language and literature at Christ Church College, likened flaneuring in the early twentieth century to a method of transcendence, solidifying romanticism in the act. In his work, *Early Modernism: Literature, Music and Painting in Europe, 1900–1916*, Butler writes, "The city's modernity is most particularly defined for him by the activities of the flâneur observer, whose aim is to derive *l'éternel du transitoire* ('the eternal from the transitory') and to see the *poétique dans l'historique* ('the poetic in the historic')." The literary critic Walter Benjamin took this idea a step further later in the twentieth century, in his collection of writings known as *The Arcades Project*. In these writings, Benjamin takes a look at the physical environment in a city and its impact on a person's spirit, with a focus on the arched tunnels, or arcades, one encounters in Paris. *The Arcades Project*, though unfinished, was a ground-breaking work that considered both the human and the environment as they impact each other.

The twentieth century is also when we finally got more female perspectives on what it meant to be a flaneur. In "The Flaneur, the Sandwichman and the Whore: The Politics of Loitering," Susan Buck-Morss, an American philosopher and intellectual historian, writes, "It is the material culture of the city, rather than the psyche, that provides the shared collective spaces where consciousness and the unconscious, past and present, meet." Buck-Morss hints that it's the physical architecture that sparks memory, both deliberate and involuntary, which is a truly beautiful thing.

Over the past couple of centuries, we've slowly but surely come to a collective understanding about flaneuring. The environment and the subject interact, creating one-of-a-kind moments that inspire and recall memories and emotions. You can't have one without the other.

With this brief overview of the history of flaneuring in mind, let's explore its evolution in greater detail.

Famous Flaneurs through History

- **Aristotle**, who led lectures while wandering with his students
- **Charles Dickens**, who walked daily after writing and when he couldn't sleep
- **Henry David Thoreau**, who found writing topics from the surroundings he discovered on walks
- **Ludwig van Beethoven**, who would run into the ocean sporadically to reenergize his work
- **Owen Wilson**, who found a time machine in the movie *Midnight in Paris*

Notice the glaring lack of women on this list? I'm leaving the following space blank so you can write in your favorite female flaneur:

- _____

Being a Flaneur in 1919 versus Being a Flaneur in 2019

Lauren Elkin, an American author living in Paris, is an expert on flaneuring. Her book *Flâneuse: Women Walk the City in Paris, New York, Tokyo, Venice, and London* is both an in-depth look at the female flaneur, or *flâneuse*, and a journey through Elkin's adventures in the many metropolises she's inhabited or visited. It also touches on the history of the struggle for gender equality in the social hierarchy of flaneuring. In Elkin's book, you'll find a treasure trove of notable women living as they want. George Sand, a name frequently mentioned throughout Elkin's book, is one great example. Sand was a brilliant French novelist lesser known by her real name: Amantine Lucile Aurore Dupin. Her work discusses free will and protests the point-blank acceptance of women submitting to their husbands, and she introduced a new group of working-class heroes to literature. As an intellectual and a woman, she defied the conventions of her time of what it meant to be a flaneur.

In *Flâneuse*, Elkin also shares anecdotes from her experience of new and old cities as a self-proclaimed flaneur, such as the tale of the understandably frustrating time when she moved to Tokyo with her boyfriend when he took a new job there. (Spoiler alert: journaling will help you get through anything—including a move gone wrong and the aftershock of losing love and learning to fall back in love with a place as a single person.) Her vision of flaneuring is one of adaptation: seeing both familiar and unfamiliar places through a new set of eyes every time she returns, mainly based on the evolving cast of loved ones who are near and far at the time.

If you're interested in digging deep into the history of female flaneurs fighting to make their voices heard, while also reading a modern take on the inner growth flaneuring can bring, I could not recommend reading Elkin's book more.

For now, let these questions I asked Elkin tide you over until you can get your hands on her work.

Q&A with Lauren Elkin

What inspired you to dive into the history of women when it comes to flaneurs?

When I started researching the figure of the *flâneuse*, I found that she was a pretty controversial figure—feminist historians couldn't agree on whether she existed or not, because women did not have ([and] still don't have) the freedom to wander in cities the way men did and do. And yet there I was—a woman who loved to walk in cities. So I decided it was important to chuck the standard definitions of a flaneur out the window and start from scratch: there have always been women in cities, and some of them must have been inspired by walking in them—what did that look like, what forms did *flâneuserie* take?

What do you think the main differences are between a woman flaneuring today versus one hundred years ago?

In cities in the global north like Paris or New York, we certainly have more freedom to go out in public on our own; a woman smoking on the street today wouldn't raise an eyebrow, but it did back then. . . .

Why do you think women were so excluded from the flaneur community at its beginnings?

For lots of reasons, depending on the situation of the women you're thinking of. But take, say, the female equivalent of the *flâneur*, who would have been a pretty middle-class guy with the leisure to hang out and observe the city. A middle-class woman would have been expected to go out accompanied. If she were on her own, she would be suspected of being of base moral character, and she would bring shame not only on herself but on her family. Women were perceived to belong to the interior, to need protection outside. It was a long fight to win our places on the sidewalk, one we're still battling to this day.

Agnès Varda is someone in your book who I found incredibly interesting. What did you find so striking about her work?

Varda is so amazing. I'm just watching her last film now, *Varda par Agnès*, and am struck all over again by the way she made these amazing films simply by looking around her and being interested in what she saw there. From *Daguerréotypes*, which is about her neighborhood in Paris, to *Mur Murs*, about the murals in Los Angeles, to *The Gleaners and I*, about people who turn up at the end of markets and "glean" the food that the vendors throw away . . . She brings this aesthetic of looking and following the thread to her films, which I think is a supremely *flâneuse*-y approach to filmmaking. I'm devastated that she's gone.

You shared some of your journal entries throughout the "Inside" chapter—do you generally keep

journals or was this something that happened as you grew more frustrated in Tokyo? If so, do you find journaling an important part of exploring a place by foot?

Great question. I've kept a journal since I studied abroad in Paris and I started writing in it during my long walks—I needed to sit down in a café and get it all down in words! I developed a real graphomania that semester, and you're right, it's totally tied to walking in the city.

If there's one thing people take away from your book, what would you hope it is?

To tune in to your surroundings, no matter what they are, urban or not. And no matter who you are, just look around you and ask, "How is this world put together?" "How is it made easier for some people to navigate than others?" "What is my responsibility in this place where I spend every day, how am I a part of it, and how do I affect other people's experiences of it?"

If you could explore any one place by foot, where would you choose?

Paris, always Paris. Any walk here is like a day in the library. I'd like to read a book about every street in Paris.

Reclaiming the Name

Someone I spoke to while I was researching this book described flaneuring in the nineteenth century quite perfectly, sharing that his own dive into the history brought up mostly mentions of "drunken, syphilitic men wandering around and allowing themselves to find romanticism or excitement or perversity." But here and now, let's kick that idea of who a flaneur is to the next planet, and then some. Everyone can romanticize a set of falling leaves on a morning walk! Women are more than capable of getting drunk and walking around! I don't mean to glorify any unhealthy moments of perversion here—emphasis on *unhealthy*—but for so long history has overlooked flaneurs who weren't a certain kind of man. Today, however, we know—and celebrate—that anyone can be a flaneur. All you need is a desire to wander.

Why Do You Walk?

Before we dive into the many ways you can flaneur today—and how you can benefit from all of the wonder, inspiration, and peace that flaneuring can bring—I want you to consider this question, because walking is arguably *the* most common, though certainly not the only, way to flaneur: *Why do you walk?*

I found myself asking this question of the people closest to me when I first started writing this book and discussing it with them—especially because being able to walk as a basic mode of transportation is a massive privilege, and it has the power to bring much more than getting in your ten thousand steps for the day. (If you can't walk, or walking is not easy for you, adjust that question to *Why do you get outside?*) Because I was so curious about how people would answer my question, I formally asked it of a small group of my friends, relatives, and colleagues. The variety of answers I received astounded me—and was also an important reminder that we all have our own priorities and reasons for going about a shared action. After I asked my interviewees why they walked, I asked each of them the same follow-up questions, which further showcased the many different reasons why someone would be inclined to get out and observe the surrounding world.

Consider the following questions a survey of sorts. Take account of your answers and be mindful of them before you set out flaneuring. Getting introspective will only help you better understand your flaneuring style.

What inspires you to get out and walk?

" I didn't realize how important walking could be in my life until I studied abroad in Rome. It was my first time in Europe (or, now that I think about it, outside the US), and I was inspired to walk everywhere as a way to get to know the city and just take it all in—the smells, the sounds, the people, the history all around. And when I moved to New York from Atlanta, which is such a car city, that same urge I felt in Rome to walk just took over. I was free from having to drive everywhere and almost never stepped foot inside of a taxi. I began walking a little more than two miles each way to work from Alphabet City to Dumbo, Brooklyn. It took me through the Lower East Side and over the Manhattan Bridge. Once on the bridge, without the threat of cars, I would take out my book and read it while walking. In Atlanta, I used to drive about a mile to work, and I remember looking back and thinking how stupid that was.

"This is my long-winded way of saying that I'm inspired to walk because it's a way to feel free, to escape the confines of a car/train/et cetera, and to really appreciate and observe your surroundings. I never walk with headphones because it takes away from the sounds and energy that're around me."

—Brooke Porter Katz, freelance writer

It would be equal parts curiosity and also a desire to get out of my own head for a little bit and just to go somewhere and be connected to an outside world."

—Joseph Gonzalez, artist and author's MVP

For me, walking helps me re-center myself during the day. I do a lot of analytical work, and it helps to get up, move around, and take a break from my computer. I usually walk for forty-five minutes to an hour in the afternoon on workdays, and then I have a ten-to-twelve-minute walk from my subway stop once I'm home. I work in West Chelsea and transferring at Times Square stresses me out, so I usually will hop off the train at Flatiron and walk to Tenth Avenue from there (it takes me about twenty minutes, but it's a way better way to start my day)."

—Emily Gregor, copy editor

"My mental health. If I'm depressed or have been indoors for too long, it's hard to be positive or not get too wrapped up in neurosis."

—Corinna Wollmann, video editor

"I started walking daily in middle school, when my parents would invite me to go on after-dinner walks. So I guess ever since then, it's become partly an after-dinner digestive aid, but also just a habit! I love going on walks in the morning, too, because the air just smells nice, and it gives me a clearheaded mind to start the day."

—Karine Hsu, cofounder of And Comfort

"My inspiration is building up my cardio and stamina so I can go on adventures. I had two knee replacements in the span of four years, and the second one wasn't as successful as the first. Getting outside and walking is harder than it used to be because of this, but my children live in cities that require a lot of walking, and I want to be able to keep up."

**—Jeanne Owen, professional retiree
and overall best mom (Hi, Mom)**

> My inspiration for walking is, when it's nice out, a nature thing for me. I love walking out in the woods—not necessarily hiking—just taking a walk in the woods because it really allows me to clear my mind. I think there's an inherent connection between us and nature that we respond to."

**—Dan Owen, professional retiree
and world-class dad (Hi, Dad)**

> I walk to work, about four miles from Clinton Hill, Brooklyn, to lower Manhattan over the Brooklyn Bridge, every morning I can—every morning I give myself enough time and the weather's nice enough. I love it because it gives me plenty of time to adjust my "mode" or my mind-set between home and work. It's relaxing and head clearing. I almost always arrive at work calm and ready for the day when I walk. It's time totally to myself. I can be thoughtful and listen to music or podcasts. It's also just great to get a bunch of fresh air and move my legs before I'll be cooped in an office all day. Also, living in New York, it can sometimes feel like you never see the actual city. You drift between your office and your home.

This allows me to walk around and really see and appreciate the city I live in—especially the amazing view over the bridge."

—Emily Johnson, e-commerce editor

66 Walking has played a lot of different roles for me over the years. It's been a way to calm anxiety, sort out thoughts, and shake ideas to the surface. I once read that Erik Satie frequently missed the last train from Paris in order to walk the several miles home, stopping under streetlights to jot down ideas. It's a romantic image that motivates me to walk when I'm feeling stuck."

—Nick Tovarek, student

66 I'm hyperaware of the privilege of being able-bodied and being able to use my able body as a *free* (!) mode of transportation. I also know how good it is for my health to move frequently, and the environmental impact that I'm negating by not driving or even using public transit. I prefer walking outside, but I've been known to walk some laps around a mall with my mom. My

mom says that the best exercise is what you enjoy, and she loves to walk, so homegirl hoofs about twenty-five K a day, too. I also really love the time that it gives me to either be alone with my thoughts and take note of the world around me in a way I wouldn't if I was driving through it, or to make phone calls to family and friends, which somehow feels much harder to do once I'm home."

—Martina Wolf Battistone, environmental planner

I walk my dog pretty much every day after work, and I plan my vacations around long hikes. I enjoy the daily walks for a few reasons. First, it gives me some exercise and time outdoors. My body just feels better on the days I walk. It also helps my mind declutter from the workday. And it gives my dog some exercise."

—Justin Sdano, IT systems administrator

Being physically active motivates me to get out and walk; how it can help not only our physical body but also mentally—it helps with cognitive function. It's our ancestral right; it's how we've always gone out to get exercise. If you think about it, the first people on Earth didn't have barbells and other things to work out with. It's always been us going out and walking, climbing different types of land in order to achieve physical goals."

**—Ryan Owen, sport-performance coach
and A+ brother (to the author)**

"Rod [my husband] and I walk because it's good for our long-term health, it keeps my blood sugars down, and gives me more energy . . . and my dog likes it, too."

**—Nicole Kriebech, CT scan technologist
and fantastic aunt (to the author)**

"I walk, a lot! [Partly] by necessity but also because I truly believe it's the best way to see everything. You miss so much from a car window. It's also why I love running. [You] can see a whole city, quickly, in a way you wouldn't be able to otherwise."

—Melissa Flynn, registered dietitian

"I actually made a move where my commute would require as much or more time walking than on the train. It kind of sucks when the weather is crummy, but I found myself walking so much more because I built the time into my commute: twenty minutes to the train each way. And you get to see things happening in your community—cafés opening, houses going on sale, people moving in—and it forces you to get fresh air. When I lived in Brooklyn, I had such a short walk to the train; it was half a block away. And because of that, I really didn't see some of the changes that were happening in my community. I mean, sure, I walked on nice days. But you don't get to know your block or neighborhood so intimately."

—Melanie Lieberman, editor

Do you prefer walking with people or solo?

66 Alone. I walk really—and I mean *really*—fast, and besides the fact that nobody can keep up with me, I prefer to have the space to get lost in my thoughts or just have some moments of peace rather than feel pressure to make conversation. The only exception is when I'm pushing my son in his stroller while he's sleeping—but even though he's there and we're connected, I still feel like I'm by myself. Walking with him is practically the reason I survived being on maternity leave."

—Brooke

66 Alone, definitely. I'm less distracted when I'm walking alone than when I'm walking with someone else."

—Joseph

" I don't actually have a preference! But I guess I prefer to walk alone in the mornings and with people at night—mostly because I treat my mornings as my me time."

—Karine

" With someone else—I like to share what I observe."

—Jeanne

" I really enjoy both walking alone and with people. I like walking by myself because it allows me to just see things for me. But if I'm walking with other people, now it's a different atmosphere. I have to be cognizant of them, what they're saying and seeing, and it's not my experience anymore. It really just depends on the people. It's always fun. I can remember when I was younger, we'd be walking downtown and it would be three or four of us walking. It was a camaraderie, it was fun. It was like a constant flow of conversation even though we weren't talking all of the time. When you're by yourself, the only conversation you have is with yourself."

—Dan

" Depends on the situation, but more so walking with people. Walking encourages conversation—healthy conversation. When Abby, my girlfriend, and I go out and walk, we have some of the best conversations of the week. We're in nature and our minds are on other things, so we can be pretty fluid with conversation. I feel like you literally cannot walk outside and be in a bad mood."

—Ryan

Do you feel better after walking outside?

" Yes, so much better. It's a way to clear my head or, if I have something on my mind, to think about how I want to deal with whatever it is. I've also drafted difficult emails in my head and written portions of articles that I'd been struggling to write while sitting in front of a computer."

—Brooke

Yes. I feel rejuvenated. Chances are I saw or heard or experienced something unique that I wouldn't have experienced had I not gone out into the world in the first place. Even on days when it's ninety-five degrees or thirty degrees, it's nice to go out and soak in that for a while and to return home. The sense of returning home is, I think, a key part of that."

—**Joseph**

I feel like a new person every time I'm able to sneak in some time outside. I try to take calls outside, as I find I'm more creative when I'm moving (and better at thinking on my feet) as opposed to when I'm sitting at my desk or in a conference room."

—**Emily**

Almost always, going out for a walk makes me feel *significantly* better."

—**Corinna**

" Absolutely. I love smelling fresh air, and there's just something about walking at my leisurely slow pace I do (which is usually plus-ten minutes from what Google Maps tells me I should be walking at) that makes me feel calm and relaxed."

—Karine

" I always feel better after walking. This is especially true when my walk involves trees, water, and animals. It's so easy to forget that we're part of an ecosystem. Walking outside is a good way to remind oneself."

—Nick

" Yes—my head feels clearer, but I'm always ready for a nap."

—Jeanne

" I always feel better when I walk outside. Sometimes it's uneventful—most of the time it's uneventful. Even if something occurs out of the ordinary, and even if it's something perceived as negative, it doesn't feel like a bad thing because you participated. You were there. If I was out walking around and I had a dog chase me, but I got away, I'd feel like kind of 'Boy, that was something.' You know what I mean? It wouldn't be fun if it caught me, but you get it. It's kind of invigorating."

—Dan

Yes, I feel *sooo* much better after walking. Calmer, happier, more alert. It gives me time to think, so I always feel like my head is full of ideas afterward."

—Emily

I can almost feel the physical weight of a bad day lifting off me during a walk home. I think it's very therapeutic. Even when it's raining, or when I'm sweating my face off in the summer, I get a rush knowing that I'm getting my steps in."

—Martina

" Absolutely. There's the science behind it: the vitamin D you're getting from the sun improves your mood and it's great for your cardiovascular health. But you have so many different things that are grabbing your attention. No matter what you're thinking about, the small stressors in your day, you turn your attention to whole-picture thinking. It adds perspective to life."

—Ryan

When you take walks, do you find yourself planning your route or enjoying the spontaneity of a place?

" It depends. If I'm under a time constraint or trying to get somewhere, I usually look it up and then take the fastest way—or if it's a place, like my office, that I go to on a regular basis, I tend to fall into a routine and stick to the streets I like best. But while living in Mexico City last year, I made an effort to be more spontaneous, especially in my neighborhood. Even if I took the most direct route to that day's coffee shop of choice, I would try to take a different way home—and luckily, it was easy where I lived because the area is filled with an abundance of winding and beautiful cobblestone streets."

—Brooke

I plan the hikes in places that have spectacular mountains, canyons, and caves. Physically, I enjoy these long hikes because they are challenging. Psychologically, these massive natural monuments make my problems and things I have been through feel so small and unimportant. I also plan a lot of the hikes to have a beautiful view at the end. I like to think this parallels life. The struggle makes you appreciate the beauty."

—Justin

Most of the time, I pick an area, like a neighborhood, and within that general area I'll just walk around with no preconceived path or direction in my head. Sometimes I'll just pick a spot to start and I'll just walk in one direction for a while. Like, I'm just going to walk up Sixth Avenue today, and I'll start at West Fourth Street and I'll finish at Thirty-Fourth Street. Pick an avenue and walk up it for a little while. I think it's easier to do that in Manhattan than it is other places, but it's one thing I do sometimes."

—Joseph

I usually have anywhere from two to seven walking routes in the neighborhoods I spend the most time in, but I'll be spontaneous in the moment. I like to have a plan, but if I find myself being drawn to another area, I go for it."

—Emily

I typically enjoy the spontaneity of a place, but once I find a few routes I really like, I'll alternate between them. I like the familiarity, that way I can really tune out, but it's also like rewatching your favorite episode of The Office . . . you start to notice details that you hadn't prior."

—Corinna

" I typically enjoy the spontaneity of a place. When I travel, I try not to get a SIM card because I love to just wander around the streets and see where I end up. Even when I'm walking my regular neighborhood route, I try to walk on different streets depending on my mood."

—**Karine**

" If I've got nowhere to be, then I happily float from whim to whim. I learned this from a dear friend who used to wake up in the morning and walk around until something happened. He always ended up in interesting situations. It's a powerful tool, but it only works if you're patient and open to new experiences."

—**Nick**

" Spontaneity—I never know where I'm going. Around here in Wisconsin, we pick an area and just start walking. When we walk, we go different ways. If we go somewhere, we just walk around to see what there is."

—**Jeanne**

" I would say that I'm probably a creature of habit with my walking routes. I guess I'm more of a practical walker than a leisurely one in that I normally have a destination. However, we recently moved to a new neighborhood, and I've experienced so much more of it by taking different streets and loops with my dog."

—Martina

" Definitely spontaneity; I wouldn't enjoy a walk that I planned. It's just like when you're traveling: You go to see something you haven't seen before, but you want to see something you didn't expect. The only way you get that is with spontaneity. Your mom and I always used to take drives in Spain without knowing where we were going. We once sat right at an empty horse-race stadium and had a picnic: sangria right on the finish line."

—Dan

" I definitely enjoy the spontaneity of a place. Usually, your day is planned for you by someone else or you plan it yourself. It's nice to take things out of your hands and just go."

—Ryan

Your Turn

Now that you've gathered some inspiration, try answering these questions yourself! The next couple of pages are for you to write down your responses.

What inspires you to get out and walk?

_____

_____

_____

_____

Do you prefer walking with people or solo?

_____

_____

_____

_____

Do you feel better after walking outside?

_____

_____

_____

_____

When you take walks, do you find yourself planning your route or enjoying the spontaneity of a place?

_____

_____

_____

_____

How to Start Flaneuring

Think of walking into a new restaurant in a foreign country where no one speaks your language. The prospect can be intimidating, but within discomfort is the potential for so much fulfillment. Walking by yourself in a new neighborhood can also create a similar sort of gut-wrenching anxiety, but I encourage you to find confidence and empowerment in no one knowing your name. Find the freedom to experience space with brand-new eyes. That certainly doesn't happen every day. And remember not to be too hard on yourself.

Simply going outside, shutting your front door, and heading in any direction makes you a flaneur. Don't make it any more complicated than it is.

You Officially Have Permission to Care Less about Your Daily Routine

I know, I know; you have places to be. And that's great! But you gain something when you start flaneuring and adjusting the way you think about getting to and from said places. Depending on other people or things to get you somewhere—public transportation, a car, or a bike—is efficient, but not always the most enjoyable.

Let's put it in perspective: There's a delay on the usual route of your morning commute—a subway malfunction or a traffic jam. Walking part of the way to your destination, or at least driving or riding the train less than you usually would, may put you where you're going a little later than you anticipated—but so will said delay. Arriving to meet your friends, starting the day at the office, or grabbing lunch at a new restaurant will be so much more enjoyable when you take the reins of your journey and leave the uncontrollable delays behind. Just by taking back the control you give to others during your daily to-and-fros, you're gaining authority of what your time looks like and taking down your daily levels of unnecessary stress . . . and who doesn't need more of that?

Once you have that nailed down, give yourself permission to care a little bit less. Before we move forward, let's define *care less*. The connotation of that phrase can come off as pretty negative. But in this case, caring less is actually giving you more space to breathe, both in a physical and mental sense. Think about how many times a day you allow your brain to do whatever it wants. Think of caring less as a gift you're giving to your brain. Take away the mental to-do lists and worries, just for a little bit, and let your thoughts do their thing.

OK, back to the big idea. Trust that in disconnecting yourself from delays and other annoyances you can't control (say, a commuter who doesn't understand the idea of personal space), you're setting yourself up for a happier trip—and then stop worrying so much. You naturally have a starting point in your flaneuring adventure, and if you have to be somewhere by a specific time, make that a goal. But don't plan so much around what happens between your start and finish. Give your brain time to flex its creativity. Those moments are just as important as the time you spend giving it tasks.

A Somewhat Long Note on the Importance of Romanticism

In the United Kingdom, some people describe themselves as roamers. Roamers are wanderers who take joy in slowing down and noticing the beauty and romance in the everyday. That could be stopping to appreciate the texture on a neighbor's concrete planter or the delicious smell wafting up from a nearby vegetable garden. On any other day, you'd walk by those things without giving them too much notice. But stopping to welcome the downright miracle that is a small plant busting up from a crack in an ancient sidewalk square will give you that warm little tingling feeling meant to remind you that beautiful things are happening without you even noticing, every day.

It's funny how focusing on small details can be a black hole of sorts. At first, a tiny struggling plant using all of its energy to produce one bloom would be considered a "tiny detail." Continue to focus on these kinds of things as you become more of a flaneur and soon you'll be taking note of the smallest deviations in paint color on a facade across the street. This kind of attention to detail sets apart the flaneur from the mall walker.

Think about your favorite storyteller. Maybe it's someone you've never met, say, master of childhood poetry Shel Silverstein, or maybe it's your best friend, who occasionally writes think pieces for an online media outlet. The one thing they probably have in common is the ability to share detail, either their own observations or vivid descriptions. Good news: you can be that person. There's a difference between "sunlit courtyard" and "courtyard bathed in golden rays, as if someone spilled a massive vial of Martha Stewart's Florentine Gold glitter and then blew it away as quickly as it appeared." If you find yourself wondering, "How do I notice details when I'm already seeing the full picture?," think of this description. And I pray to whichever gods or goddesses may exist that I someday find you wandering around Brooklyn muttering under your breath, "Martha Stewart's Florentine Gold glitter."

Beginner Tips

Trying any new activity can feel weird at first. But you can do a few things to make sure flaneuring fits into your life as seamlessly as possible. You know how the old saying goes: a habit that's easy and better than battling rush-hour crowds is a habit you'll keep!

1. Invest in a good pair of shoes. Yes, I'm telling you to buy new shoes. See? Flaneuring is already *so fun*. You want some good foot support when you're walking around, and when you're off on a wandering spree, you never know what you're going to encounter. Turn-of-the-century cobblestone? Not good for heels! Unpaved walkways? Sandals are out. Take care of your feet, friends.

2. Take breaks. This isn't a marathon; if you find a place you especially like, spend some time taking it all in. To help encourage this kind of break, pack a snack.

While it does add a to-do to your flaneuring session, the only rule is "stop to eat something." And that kind of directive is the most fun kind of directive.

3. Turn it into a game. Only take right turns. Make a turn every time you see someone wearing a red shirt/coat/sweater. Pop into every bookstore you see and read one page from five different books.

4. Know when to stop. This is easy if you have a final destination. If not, give yourself a time limit. Walk for an hour and then find your way home. If you're short on time, walk in one direction and take every second right turn. You'll find yourself back in your original setting pretty quickly, but you'll become more familiar with your surrounding environment.

5. Fight boredom. If you feel yourself losing interest, make it a point to find the most banal item or scene in your current line of sight. Find something beautiful about it. Sometimes your brain needs a vague task to get the creative juices flowing. If you're prone to doo-dling, bring out your notebook and pencil and try your hand at capturing the thing. If you're more of a word-smith, write a goofy haiku about it or settle on three words to describe it. If nothing else, walking by the same area will bring a smile to your face just in remem-bering your attempts at turning something incredibly basic into something fun. And that's a win.

6. Write it all down. This is a great rule for anything in life. Think about how excited (or possibly mortified) you would be to discover a box full of journals perfectly preserving your memories and feelings from when you were a teenager. Now just think of how cool it could be to come across a box of journals from your daily walks a decade prior, a key that opens a door to what your neighborhood or city used to look like. You could use these diaries as a guide to retake those walks, trying to identify the same spots or objects you saw the first time and noting differences now. We're getting ahead of ourselves, but it's always fun to imagine that your efforts today will be a delightful surprise in your future.

Safety Tips for Flaneurs

A lot of factors will determine how accessible flaneuring out in the world is for you. While gender can still be an issue for flaneurs, given that catcalling is unfortunately very much alive, race also plays an important role. Being a white woman, I don't experience flaneuring as a black woman of my age would, just as a Puerto Rican woman of my age wouldn't share the same experiences as me, despite us all having uncomfortable stories to tell.

If you're interested in knowing more about one black woman's experience exploring her hometown of Toronto, check out Jacqueline L. Scott's blog, *Black Outdoors*. In an especially insightful post called "A Black Flaneur in the 'Hood," Scott shares her thoughts on a woman's role at midlife, out of the radarlike zone of the male gaze, and compares them to her own experiences as a flaneur who is also a black woman. I highly recommend reading the essay in full.

In the post, Scott digs into the dangers of putting yourself on display in certain regions and countries, and in doing so she makes an important point: in our present political and cultural climate, it's simply not safe for some people to walk in certain places. While I wish I—or anyone else—could make the world safe for all flaneurs, I'm sharing some tactics for staying safe when out flaneuring based on my own experiences. Let me be the first to remind you: I am a young white woman. If you want to better understand how someone of a different race, gender, or sexual orientation keeps safe while flaneuring, I encourage you to read the experiences of others or to talk to them. Listen to them and broaden your understanding of the world. In the meantime, here are a few of my own tips for staying as safe as possible while exploring.

Know Your Physical Early-Warning Signs

When it comes to safety, Scott pays attention to the hairs on the back of her neck. "They are my early warning racial radar," she writes on her blog. This is another great point Scott brings up: no matter who you are and especially if you're a woman or a person of color, it's important to identify your early-warning reactions. We all have them, whether it's the hair on the back of our neck standing straight up or that feeling that someone is watching us, despite our being in a relatively empty space. Listen to your body and be aware of how you feel.

Tell Someone Where You're Walking

Even if you don't know exactly where you'll be wandering, let a buddy know your general area, especially if you're heading somewhere new. Another option is to share your location with a family member or partner on Google Maps. And before you go all "Where's the privacy?!" on me, remember that you can turn your location sharing on and off. My partner and I share our locations with each other, especially given that he's known to disappear for a day on his bike somewhere north of New York City. Share a general return time with your roommate so he or she will know when to start getting worried, if need be.

Wear Bright Colors If Flaneuring at Night

Just as if you're riding a bike alongside cars, make sure to wear some reflective clothing. You want to be certain people can see you as you're crossing the street, hiking along a path, or, of course, riding a bike.

Research New Spaces

Researching a general area doesn't mean you have to choose your route ahead of time. But you should know what kind of area you'll be wandering in. For example, college campuses are great places to explore, while industrial lots may be less fun and potentially dangerous. A quick look at the satellite view on Google Maps will give you a good feel for where you're heading. And if you're really worried about potentially stepping into an unwelcoming neighborhood, try heading into nature.

Bring a Buddy

The first time I walked to work, I asked one of my closest friends, Laura, to walk with me. I knew my final destination and a general direction to travel, but I wanted to bring along someone I trusted—and also loved to chat with—to walk with me on that first go. Not only did we have a great time, but the walk flew by. This time, I wasn't as worried about neighborhoods (I'm very familiar with downtown Brooklyn and lower Manhattan), but more so just anxious to put myself out there. Bringing someone into the experience with you takes so much of the pressure off. Make sure to explain what flaneuring is to your walking buddy before you take off; there's nothing worse than trying to observe your surroundings with someone who has no interest in doing so.

Know Your Limits

Just as with any other kind of exercise, know what your physical limits are. If you're experiencing sharp pain in your feet versus the general throb that comes with a long walk, take a break. You may not be a doctor, but you know when you're doing something your body doesn't like. Listen to your body, especially, if you're flaneuring in an area that's physically demanding. Hiking can go from enjoyable stroll to scary scramble quickly, depending on where you are. Never be afraid to take a step back. As soon as you stress your body, your mind is more focused on the nerve-racking task at hand and not on experiencing your environment as a flaneur should.

If walking is not in the cards for you, adjust the process a bit. You can flaneur from the comfort of a chair or leaning up against a tree. The main thing is that you're gifting your attention to the outward scene instead of inward to your thoughts. Just make sure you've got the proper sun protection if you are going to be sitting outside for a long time. A sunburned flaneur is not a good look.

Pod Plays and Audio Walks

If the idea of flaneuring intrigues you but also makes you a bit nervous because you don't know where to start, stick with me. You can take baby steps to get into the flaneuring habit. Take it slow, and instead of asking your friends for places to walk, things to see, experiences to try, take some advice from an experienced stranger. It's not as scary as it sounds (promise!).

Audio Walks

These are exactly what they sound like: walks that are guided by prerecorded audio. Janet Cardiff, a Canadian artist who does some incredible work with sound installations, transforms the taking-in of a particular space through her audio walks. These force you to use all of your senses to their most acute levels and place you in the center of reality, while adding another layer of storytelling that will have you second-guessing your perceptions.

Cardiff's most famous work might be *Her Long Black Hair*, which you can experience in New York City's Central Park. The goal of *Her Long Black Hair* is to put you as in-scene as possible in the park. Cardiff guides you from location to location with her voice, prompting you to look at specific photos as the walk progresses. The result is two story lines: the one playing out around you and the one being fed into your ear by Cardiff. This audio walk will take you thirty-five minutes, winding you through the iconic lawns to the tune of a psychological story line. Originally, one listened to the audio files on a CD player, and a package of photos was given to each participant. Today, you can download the audio files from the Public Art Fund website and check out the photos on your phone. Another NYC must-visit: *The Forty Part Motet* at MoMA PS1 in Long Island City, which is an art installation comprised of forty speakers, arranged in the shape of an oval, that each play a unique recording of a person singing. Cardiff has other work if you don't live in or plan on visiting New York City anytime soon. She's created walks through the Villa Medici, a Renaissance-style palace in Rome, and through an old train station in Kassel, Germany. If you're looking to really dive into the mind of someone who lives and breathes the relationship between people and the sounds around them, Cardiff has even written a book on her experiments in sound and video titled *The Walk Book*.

Pod Plays

First thing's first: If you've never heard the word "pod play" before, don't fret. This is supposed to be easing you into the world of flaneuring, remember? Think of a pod play as a podcast that's directing you to do something—and more often than not asking you to walk in a certain direction. There is a destination at the end of the pod play; you just don't quite know what it is when you start off, in most cases.

Matt Sosin, creator of the Los Angeles–based pod play Drift—and from here on out, my heart and soul are referring to Matt as "Papa Pod Play"—has his own spin on flexing your sense of reality. Similar to Cardiff's audio walks, Drift will allow participants to follow along on a journey that adds another dimension to our tactile world; this time, by introducing locals and tourists to magical places around Los Angeles. "I started being exposed to the medium a few years ago through immersive theater and site-specific performance work,"

Sosin told me. "That led me to pod plays, and I wanted to make one in Los Angeles. I did some research and couldn't find any that lived in the city." Sosin partnered with various government agencies in Los Angeles, including the tourism board, to help do just that. "My interest was creating something that anybody could access continuously moving forward; a story that lived in a space that had the live element of the world—which is why I love theater—but also involves a prerecorded element. The really wonderful part of pod plays for me are these magic moments where you're listening to something that you know is prerecorded, but that lines up with a real-life thing happening in the space that somehow tangentially correlates to something. You know, you'll hear a child laughing to your right, and you'll see maybe a child not laughing or something weird like that." But it's much more than a blip in your reality. It's bringing actual magic to your day.

"A lot of the sites I focused on are areas that people don't go to," Sosin said. "They aren't necessarily labeled as tourist attractions. One of the sites is a cross street in South Pasadena: East Fair Oaks and Washington Avenue, where the largest roost of Mexican parrots exists. They're an endangered species, and this is the second-largest population in the world. . . . Every evening, about ten minutes before sunset until ten minutes after sunset, they come home to sleep. There are thousands of these birds in the air . . . the sound is all around you. It's extremely powerful. It was mind-boggling to me that this wasn't a thing on lists for people to go and do and see."

Don't let the newness or uncertainty of flaneuring turn you off from a lifetime of adventures. Once you take that first step out of your comfort zone, whether figuratively or literally, you'll realize how easy it is to make flaneuring a part of your daily routine. When you get the hang of it, you won't even consciously realize that you're flaneuring while doing so. Taking the long way, the scenic route, whatever you want to call it, will become second nature. You'll know you've developed a knack for flaneuring when your friends start praising you for "being able to fit into any situation."*

---

* Actual words I've dreamed of my friends saying.

How to Flaneur Every Day

The odds are that I woke up this morning mad at the sun for rising earlier than I wanted it to. That is not a good way to start the day. In my experience, if the morning or before work is the only time you have to do some flaneuring, you'll likely have to get up a bit earlier than you're used to. If you're one of those blessed people who already find yourself rising before your alarm, well . . . more power to you. But if you're like me, you will have to force yourself out of the house / apartment / dorm room / van / place with a bed earlier than you're ready to leave. And I mean force yourself.

Even if you aren't stepping out in the morning, leaving the comfort of home can be hard. Realize this and make a conscious effort to get excited about the unknown. The real intrigue of being a flaneur comes from one thought and one thought only: you never know what joyful discovery you're going to make. It only takes my making eye contact with one adorable dog to counteract the annoyance of rushing myself out the door for a few minutes of aimless wandering before I need to head to the office. Flaneuring doesn't have to be only a weekend or day-off-work activity. Those are both good times to start—especially when you're still unsure about the idea—but finding small ways to incorporate flaneuring into your daily life can make you a happier person.

Dissect Your Daily Routine

If there's one way to throw yourself into flaneuring, it's with the activity we're about to outline in this section. Remember, the goal of this exercise is to identify the parts of your daily to-dos that you'd like to improve upon. This is a good thing. If you feel yourself getting annoyed or overwhelmed with the number of things you discover you do every day, just remember you're doing this to make your days more enjoyable.

Here we go. Start by writing down all of the elements of what "getting ready for the day" means in your life. Circle the not-so-fun parts. Can you improve any of those by getting outside and setting aside some time to romanticize what you may previously have found mundane? If you can, let go of the pressure that comes with a routine and celebrate the rituals. Just as making pour-over coffee can bring joy to your morning, getting off one subway stop early and walking to work can also bring that same bliss. So, go ahead, care less about the train delay you can't control. Don't let road rage bring you down. Pick a new album to listen to, plug in, and start walking.

If you need a template for putting your routine on paper, let me help a bit. This is what my routine looks like on any given Friday (aka the best day that ever was and ever will be):

Wake Up! You're Going to Be Late:[*] 6:00 a.m.

Actual Time I Woke Up: 6:35 a.m.[†]

Get Dressed / Shower / Brush Teeth / Become
    Presentable: 6:35 a.m.–7:15 a.m.

Commute to Personal Training Session:[‡] 7:15 a.m.–
    7:30 a.m.

Move Too Much (i.e., Work Out): 7:30 a.m.–8:30 a.m.

Commute to Work: 8:30 a.m.–9:15 a.m.

---

[*] This is what my alarm is named on my iPhone.

[†] I know. Life is hard.

[‡] I'm usually running late and frantically calling an Uber.

Work Too Much:[*] 9:15 a.m.–6:30 p.m.

Eat Lunch or Something Resembling Lunch: Between
12:30 p.m. and 1:30 p.m.

Commute Home: 6:30 p.m.–7:15 p.m.

Eat Dinner: Between 7:30 p.m. and 9:00 p.m.

Write / Work on Freelance Projects: Between 9:00 p.m.
and midnight

Rinse and Repeat F o r e v e r

The things I circled on my list because they are "not-so-fun" were Commute to Personal Training Session, Commute to Work, Work Too Much, and Commute Home. Notice a pattern? You've probably already guessed, but I think the New York City subway is the worst place in the world. I don't mean to bash the MTA; I am just strongly dissatisfied with this common way of getting around the city. For you to truly understand where I'm coming from, let me explain my average commute when I don't walk to work. I'll leave my apartment

---

[*] Alternate title: "Emails, Emails, Emails."

about forty-five minutes before I want to be sitting at my desk. I walk about two minutes to the nearest G train station and ride for a few stops before I transfer to another train that I ride for a few stops, which will eventually drop me off in the new-and-improved Fulton Station in Tribeca. My morning commute is usually filled with weird food smells, the occasional spilled coffee (sometimes on my shoes), and cranky people who are forced to stand entirely too close to one another on a delayed train. It's not fun or glamorous, despite what my high school friends may think based on the Instagram DMs they send me.

I also often find myself in an uncharacteristically dark place during my winter commutes. I'm talking "darker than a subway car after its lights flicker out while stuck in the middle of a tunnel underneath the East River" dark. So when I sat down to think about the aspects of my day I could revitalize by incorporating some flaneuring into my daily routine, I thought of the wonderful little invention with two wheels.

I love riding my bike—most of my free time on the weekends is spent riding around with my partner, who inspired my cycling. (We once lived in a smaller-than-small studio apartment and prioritized fitting three bikes inside instead of a table to eat dinner at.) However, for convenience I usually chose the subway over my bike during the week. A lot of things kept me from riding my bike to work: the fear of riding over a tourist-choked bridge, getting nicked by a car on a busy street, not being able to find a safe spot to lock up—the list went on. While it seemed like a lot of work in the beginning, and admittedly it is, the eventual payoff was my being able to leave the crowded, stressful subway to everyone else.

I determined that becoming more comfortable with my route to work—or the various routes I could take, in keeping with the flaneur spirit—would make it possible to avoid the subway during days with bikeable weather. See? That wasn't too bad. Writing down the parts of your daily routine that could be improved through flaneuring makes them a lot less anxiety inducing.

Take a few minutes and try doing it yourself.

_____

_____

_____

_____

_____

_____

_____

_____

Done? If I could give you a cookie, I would.

Flaneuring Your Daily Routine

Once you've identified the parts of your daily routine that can be flaneured, it's time to just do it. Don't let your having a final destination throw you off the flaneuring path. Familiarize yourself with the various routes that will get you there, and let yourself spontaneously choose your route as you walk.

A quick note on spontaneity. It is so much harder than it sounds. If you think about what the brain is doing all day, it's avoiding chaos and seeking control. Flaneuring by nature is giving up a bit of control. Keep this awareness somewhere in your brain and in no time you'll find yourself succumbing to the sweet, sweet strolls of an aimless wanderer.

I made the "just-do-it" decision to walk to work on a particularly nice day, and I found that not only was it a great way to get my steps in and get outside, which is an act of love in itself for my mental health, but it also ended up banishing all of the things I hated about my typical commute: train delays and annoying commuters with no sense of personal space. Here are some things I noticed while on this walk and after:

1. I saw a lot of people smile. I'm sure these people were mainly tourists who don't understand the frustration of having to head to work in New York City on a beautiful spring day, but that doesn't *really* matter. It made me happy.

2. The morning light bouncing off the Brooklyn Bridge was completely enchanting. I popped in my headphones to drown out the constant honk of car horns and just watched how the light slipped through the various beams and supports of the bridge. I spent a few minutes trying to figure out how the bridge fit together, which steel beams held each other up. I tried to count all of the different shapes I found in the structure: circles, triangles, squares, rectangles, lines, alphabets. Giving in to a game of internal I Spy before 10 a.m. is something I'd recommend to anyone.

3. Overhearing more than fifty separate conversations in one morning might just be the best way to come up with a movie script. All the stories spiderwebbed together, but the sound bites of the Brooklyn Bridge at 8:00 a.m. is a soundtrack I'd listen to any day.

4. I found a new favorite breakfast food: *migas* taco. I got hungry about twenty minutes into my walk and, lo and behold, there stood Hungry Ghost, one of my favorite pop-in Brooklyn coffee chains. I had the hard choice between a ham-and-cheese croissant (classic) or a *migas* breakfast taco (craving). When I don't know what to do, I generally ask the person physically closest to me. On this sunny morning in downtown Brooklyn, it was the barista. I applaud him for taking more than thirty seconds to give me an answer, and he even threw in a question ("Have you ever *had* a *migas* taco before?" Answer: "No"). Hats off to baristas who hustle. Anyway, I had the taco. And I immediately fell in love with a new morning snack.

5. It was prime people-watching time. The human face can contort in interesting ways when it's frustrated at a car passing too closely or at a crosswalk light that doesn't seem to be moving at optimal speed. The best way to view these faces is directly across said crosswalk with the morning light bouncing off the grimaces of commuters in a hurry. I say this part in jest, but mostly in awe of how everyone can look completely different. One interesting thing that's happened since I started walking around more is that my dreams have filled with more faces. I may not remember them when I wake up, but from what I do remember, my dream scenarios are always in public, crowded places and full of facial details. Riddle me that, Rorschach.

6. I had more energy and my head felt clearer going into the workday. One of my favorite things about doing more walking early in the morning has become the perspective it brings to my day. Watching everyone's universe pass one another on the street is a great reminder that any stress that's presented to you throughout the day is not the end of the world. So many other people out there are having a rough day; something about *seeing* so many other people in person drives that idea home. Remember, you're not saving lives . . . unless, of course, you are. Most likely, the thing that's stressing you out isn't worth the emotional effort you're giving it. On the days when I walk to work now, it's easier to remember that.

Flaneuring When You Don't Live in a Big City

While my most recent adventures as a self-proclaimed flaneur have happened in a city, I am a Midwestern girl at heart. I grew up in Wisconsin, where finding a hidden location in a cornfield to sneak a bottle of low-alcohol wine or schnapps turned so many of my friends into teenage flaneurs. I don't recommend doing that (especially if you're underage!), but you have so many ways to incorporate flaneuring into your life when you live in an area without public transportation or even a Main Street.

Get Thee to a National Park

Some of the best places for flaneuring are national parks. If you think about it, they're pretty much a playground for anyone looking to spend some time wandering the Great Outdoors. Given that high-trafficked parks generally come with frequent visitor centers, you can give yourself the freedom to let go without worrying about getting dangerously lost. Just make sure you have the right footwear if hiking is in your future.

If you don't live near a national park and getting to one seems more like a pricey vacation than a simple hike, do some research on nearby state parks and local nature preserves. If those are nonexistent, head to the nearest botanical garden. Places such as these are designed to encourage wandering, despite clear walking paths.

Winter Activities Are for (Flaneuring) Lovers

Snowshoeing, snowmobiling, skiing, skating—all of these are S-words and all are great opportunities for flaneuring. Sure, the Midwest and Northern states (and any area that isn't a metropolis such as New York or Los Angeles) may not have as many skyscrapers or bustling urban neighborhoods with a seemingly infinite amount of things to see and do. But these areas have incredible natural environments. While the winters in many of these places can be brutal, this season can also be the best time of year to get outside and take in gorgeous scenery—as well as combat your seasonal depression.

Getting outside in the winter months is a great activity to do with a buddy, considering freezing temperatures and large snowfalls can create potentially dangerous situations. That said, walking around in the wintertime doesn't mean you have to spend the entire time alongside someone else. Take advantage of the deep quiet that freshly fallen snow brings. Tell your buddy you need a bit of solo time, pick a direction, and find a good place to do some contemplating. It's amazing how much calmer a winter tundra can make the brain. Just take care to bundle up and have the right gear (more on that later in this chapter).

Downtown "City Name Here"

Whatever your town deems its downtown area can be a prime spot for flaneuring. Start on one end of the downtown area and weave your way through to the other side. Don't limit yourself to any one activity. If you want a drink, hop into a nearby café or bar. If you're hungry, grab a snack. Need a rest? Find a bench. Need some quiet time? Find the local library and wander through its rows of bookshelves.

Take special note of all the things you've never noticed before: the shape of a street sign, the lack of a curb on a particular stretch of road, the strong smell of chlorine outside the local pool, how sad a playground looks around sunset without any children climbing all over it. It's funny how a place so familiar to you can take on different personalities throughout the day. This is another great time to keep a flaneur journal: when you're exploring a place you practically know by heart. Being able to find new meaning and beauty in the places you see every day is a wonderful thing.

Your Local Supercenter

If a Walmart or a Costco is all you've got available as a safe space for mindful wandering, work with it. Leaving a shopping list at home is usually not advisable, but fight the urge to shop for anything. Loop through the aisles taking note of the never-ending products and options and think about overconsumerism . . . or don't.

Maybe you're in it for the people-watching. If you're a design enthusiast, pay special attention to all of the brand logos or labels you see. Find your favorite. Find the worst one. Imagine a world where Nabisco made furniture or Florida's Natural provided health care.

While flaneuring is about reveling in the mundane, a side effect is that it can also help calm your mind. You might find it hard getting into the right headspace when you're surrounded by fluorescent lights and families following a grocery list, so consider this a task in meditation (something we'll dive even deeper into in the chapter "Flaneuring as Meditation"). If you feel yourself getting distracted or anxious, focus on your breathing, pretend you can feel the stress leaving each part of your body one spot at a time, and give yourself one of the prompts above (my go-to is finding my favorite and least-favorite labels). Think of it this way: you can treat yourself to a pint of ice cream or a chocolate bar after you've had enough. Oh, the joys of being an adult on the road to personal betterment. . . .

The Farmers' Market

During the summertime—and fall and spring—your local farmers' market can be the ultimate destination for flaneuring. Since what's available usually transitions with the seasons, you never know what you're going to find. Plan a flaneur's dinner and buy your groceries at the market. Purchase whatever speaks to you, not ingredients for any specific recipe. Buy a handful of heirloom tomatoes because the color reminds you of your girlfriend's cheeks after a long day of bike riding. Give in to your urge to head home with some vibrant green scallions just because they were the brightest things on the table. And never hold back from buying yourself fresh flowers. Ambience is just as important as the plate in front of you.

The farmers' market is also a fantastic place to observe the people around you. Visit one on a weekend and you'll find friends and partners catching up, swapping stories, and making plans. Feed off the weekend fever everyone around you is indulging in . . . then grab an apple-cider doughnut or whatever snack is calling your name and find a bench. Even flaneurs need a break.

To err on the side of budget safety, give yourself a certain amount of money you can spend at the farmers' market—and do yourself a favor and take out cash. It will not only help you keep track of how much you're spending, but local vendors usually prefer it to cards.

Flaneuring While Driving

Let's temporarily adjust our definition of *flaneur* from "aimless wanderer on the hunt for beauty in the mundane" to include "paying close attention to the road, but still taking the scenic route" for this section. (Seriously, please pay attention when you drive!) If driving is easier for you than walking, and you're interested in some flaneuring, then drive new routes and try flaneuring while driving.

I grew up near a lake so I have many memories of the thrill of late-night swims with friends and family. Whenever I go home, which is not nearly enough, I make a point to borrow my parents' car (wow, that phrase brings back . . . memories) and drive around the neighborhood. I don't plan which streets I'm going to take, and I don't put a time limit on it. Sometimes I stop and walk around, and sometimes I don't. I always try to set out around sunset, and that's my only parameter— all of the winding roads end up pushing you off on one of the surrounding main roads anyway. Giving yourself a moment to relive your memories, alone, and revisit a place from your childhood is truly a trip. I don't think I've ever even told my parents or brother what I'm doing when I head out, which somehow makes it even more special—though I have to assume they've got an idea. It's nice to have something noteworthy you can enjoy every time you return home. For example, here's a special memory I indulged in on a recent scenic drive back home:

The last time I drove around my childhood neighborhood, I decided on a whim to park near the entrance to the small lake about a three-minute drive from our house. To get there, you have to drive down a hill we called Killer Hill, which my father once drove a riding lawn mower down by accident and somehow didn't hurt himself, and then down a number of winding tree-lined roads. You would miss the lake entrance if you weren't actively looking for it. It's a small gravel pull-off on the right side of the road a couple of hundred feet before the area's main campground, right on the water's edge.

When I was younger, the lot—which is only big enough to fit three small cars, max—was constantly bustling with fancy rides from the Chicago families that rented homes in the area for the summer. In the wintertime, you'd find local vehicles parked while their drivers walked down to the water to look for a quiet spot to enjoy the scenery. On the day I visited, the lot was completely empty; the pull-off's gate was closed to anyone trying to get in. The small lot is surrounded by trees, and the single Porta Potti was almost completely covered in vines. A series of steps leads you to a small dock, the spots of which are auctioned off to locals hoping they'll someday have a reason to buy a pontoon or a small rowboat. I hopped out of the car and walked to the end of the dock, remembering how unstable it was when I got a running start to cannonball into the water. I sat, dipped my feet in the water, and read a few pages of a Nora Roberts novel my mom had left in the car. I was instantly reminded of a time I decided to study for a high school chemistry exam . . . on the floating pavilion about thirty feet from the dock. Teenage Erika's solution included running home to grab a large-enough Tupperware container to fit my giant book and swimming it over to the sunbathing deck, as we called it when I was younger. Let that ingenious tactic sink in for a minute before I tell you that I had to pay a fine for water damage when I returned the book. Memories are a wild thing. This experience is something I haven't thought about since it happened, and recalling it warmed my heart. So encourage your mind to wander; visit a familiar place and remember the person you were when it was the most familiar to you.

This is another instance that's great for bringing along a notebook. I would never have remembered that event even if someone had for some destined reason uttered the words "put a textbook in a Tupperware container" in a single sentence. Something about being alone at the dock at sunset and reading a few pages of a book that had been forgotten in my parents' car brought the scene forward from the deepest vault of my seemingly unimportant memories. I wrote it down in my phone's notes app, which is the only reason I'm sharing it with you here. In my most vulnerable moments of impostor syndrome at work, the memory lights up my day when I'm wondering what my teenage self would think of the work I'm doing now.

Do yourself a favor and start keeping notes, whether

it's physically in a notebook or in an app. You never know when you'll need a reminder that Younger You was pretty darn special, or a "fun fact" for a rousing set of icebreaker games.

All of this is to say, don't underestimate the power of taking the scenic route. If driving around for an undetermined amount of time makes you nervous for both yourself and the environment, set some boundaries. Commit to stopping after every fifteen minutes of drive time. Once you hit fifteen minutes, give yourself four minutes to find a good spot to stop. Get out, stretch your legs, go for a walk, sit on a particularly comfortable-looking patch of grass. Flaneuring while driving is just a means for getting out of your daily bubble and into a different version of yourself.

Flaneuring for Exercise

Another way to incorporate flaneuring into your daily routine is to do it while you're exercising. If you're already outside running, for instance, you can easily add a few new techniques to your routine as a means of infusing more of the flaneuring spirit into your runs. Into cycling? Easy. Even if you frequent group fitness classes, there are ways to flaneur while getting your heart rate up.

Flaneuring for Runners

A daily run can double as flaneuring. Take new streets, ask friends for their favorite run routes, drive out of your hometown and run in a new park. Think of a fun shape and draw it out on a map; try to stick to those lines while you're on your run. Any of these things will put you in a semi-new environment, making it even easier to notice the subtle details all around you.

One thing to keep in mind: Safety is always going to come first, and you should have a general idea of where you're running and how far you are from home. Try to plan your runs for the daytime, and tell someone where you're going if you're trying a new route. If you want to track your distance and route, look for an app that does this for you. Strava is a great option—marketed as an app for all athletes, it will not only track your run, but it will also show you your friends' routes and stats, if you're looking for inspiration.

Create a group of like-minded running flaneurs and dedicate yourselves to planning a new route every week. Not only are you finding safety in numbers, but running is always more fun when you can hide in the middle of a crowd (at least for me).

Flaneuring for Cyclists

Cycling is even easier to incorporate flaneuring into than running. Again, you'll want to map out a general route—or at least a neighborhood or region you want to stick to—but aside from that, I encourage you to take new roads to get wherever you're going.

Take that advice—to find new roads—to mean "do

your research." Know where your bike lanes are; find out when rush hour is and where it hits the hardest and if any roads are closed. While you'll always correct your path when on a bike to avoid traffic, crowds, and boring roads, it's better to have a good idea of which turns won't get you anywhere.

Flaneuring for Gym Rats

If most of your workouts are indoors, try walking to or from the gym. If you don't have enough time to get the whole way by foot, park farther from the gym and walk the rest of the way. Consider it a preworkout mind-clear. Not only will it help you get some fresh air, but it might also force you to wake up a tad earlier if you attend morning classes. Nothing is worse than waking up super-late before a workout, not to mention that you'll completely ignore your surroundings when you're in a mad dash to get sweaty.

If you're crunched for time in getting to your class,

set aside some postworkout time for your flaneuring. There's no better way to cool down than aimlessly walking around the block.

Flaneuring for Fitness-Class Fans

If you typically attend workout classes with a friend or group of friends, try adding to the agenda a brisk walk before your class. Not only can you use this walk to catch up with your pals, but you can also spend some time appreciating everything around you before your intense workout session.

Dressing for Flaneuring Success . . . No Matter How Cold It Is

To flaneur properly every day, you've got to dress the part. Nothing is more annoying than realizing ten minutes into a walk that you didn't wear enough layers. You can always remove a layer, but you can't put one on that isn't with you. Here's a quick checklist for every season, no matter where you live or may be traveling.

Spring

Start with a base layer, whether it's a tank top or a merino-wool turtleneck (think California versus Iceland for those extremes). Top it with a sweater (extra points if it's a zip-up you can easily remove). I bought a funnel-neck sweater from Lou & Grey a few years ago that has quickly become my go-to walking sweater. It's light enough that it doesn't send me into a sweaty tizzy once the sun comes out, but blocks the wind if it decides to blow. The sweater is also loose enough to wear with something underneath . . . and it's super-cute.

Pack a waterproof windbreaker if you've got one. As a simple guideline, you should be able to fit this into a backpack or purse without adding any annoying weight onto your shoulders.

Summer

What a joy it is to be able to walk outside in a T-shirt and shorts. Unless you live in a Nordic region where summer temperatures max out around sixty degrees Fahrenheit, you'll be most comfortable in breathable clothing and shoes. If I'm heading out on a longer jaunt, I tend to wear my Nike Flyknits because you don't have to wear socks with them, they've got great airflow, and they named my shoe style after one of my best friends (Mariah). #Priorities.

During the summer, absolutely do not forget a water bottle, hat, and sunscreen. More sunscreen than you think you'll ever need. If you're an especially fair-skinned flaneur, play it safe and wear a hat.

Fall

Think of falltime flaneuring like springtime flaneuring, but with a slightly heavier jacket. You can probably ditch the waterproof layer as long as you check the weather. Flannel goes a long way when you're venturing out in the fall—wear a tank top with a flannel button-up over it and chances are you're good to go. Pair that with jeans and solid hiking or walking boots, and take that hike!

Winter

As I've previously mentioned, winter can be a great time to flaneur, but it's especially important then to dress the part. Do yourself a favor and find a pair of waterproof pants to wear in place of your regular pants. Wear a base layer underneath with some high woolen socks. You're going to need some heavier-duty boots, especially if you live where giant snowfall is a *thing*. Always bring a scarf. Those single-use hand-warmer things (you know, the ones your mom or dad or who-ever loves you the most is always sending you in care packages) should be your best friends. Thanks, Mom.

The Art of the Picnic

As with anything else—studying, eating, reading, listening to Brazilian jazz—some people can handle more than others. The same goes for flaneuring. It's not just about your physical stamina—it's also about your concentration. If you already have a short attention span, adding hunger to that can wreak havoc on your jaunt.

I recommend occasionally packing a snack (or five) for flaneuring. I think picnics are the most underrated summer activity. For many reasons picnics make for the best dining experience: You get to pick out a cute blanket; it's an excuse to eat all of your favorite foods; when you get full, you can literally lie down for a nap (a very encouraged picnicking activity); and dining alfresco cannot be beat. Not to mention, you can buy picnic kits with adorable plates, bowls, cups, and silverware all in a (hopefully wicker) carrying case. You don't need a partner to pack a picnic, either. If you picnic solo, there's more snacking for you. Be a little selfish . . .

unless you *are* flaneuring with someone, then you've got to share. If you need some help deciding what to bring on your adventure, here are some of the best foods for a flaneur's picnic:

Apples

McIntosh, Honeycrisp, Granny Smith, Braeburn—it doesn't matter what variety you're eating; it's going to be one of the most refreshing things you can do while flaneuring. If you're flaneuring in the fall, try to get your hands on some apple cider or apple-cider doughnuts. If you find yourself flaneuring in a farmers' market during the fall, you'll likely easily find some of these treats.

Cookies

Pick your favorite and make a batch the night before you set off flaneuring, or buy your favorite brand from the store (I prefer Tate's chocolate chip cookies).

Cucumber Salad

Cut up slices of cucumbers and douse them in vinegar, cold water, and a mix of your preferred herbs and spices—I like lots of salt, a touch of dill, and a tiny dash of Aleppo pepper—in a Tupperware container. Do this right before you head out and your cucumbers will be deliciously marinated by the time you sit down to enjoy them.

Sandwiches

There is no better food for a flaneur than a sandwich. Sandwiches are perfect if you're keen on eating as you walk. The beauty of a sandwich is that you can put whatever you want between those two slices of bread. Free yourself from your sandwich shackles! Craving bananas, Nutella, and peanut butter? You do the damn thing! Got leftover caprese from last night's dinner? Put it in a sandwich!

Fresh Fruit

You are so great and deserve your own fruit salad. Grab your favorite fruits from the grocery store—I usually make a beeline for pineapple, mango, apples, and grapes. Cut them up at home, and pack yourself a picnic. The best thing about a fruit salad is that you can eat it in stages. The longer you wait, the more the fruits will mix and marry their juices (sorry, I fully realize that's a gross sentence and here I am, torturing you), making it even more delicious.

Lemonade

Water is good—great even—considering it's necessary to live. You should drink water while flaneuring. But you can also bring along something that's more delicious, if you have room to carry it. Fool everyone and fill a flask, or a regular old water bottle, with some lemonade for a sweet treat midwalk.

Egg Salad

Egg salad is highly underrated, and it's just as good in a sandwich as it is straight from a bowl with a bit of salt and pepper. Make it the night before and add a few dashes of hot sauce if you're looking for an extra kick. It's also easy to whip up a large batch of egg salad, which makes it a great option if you're flaneuring with a crowd.

Almonds

Almonds are one of the healthiest and most efficient snacks. They're even easier than sandwiches to eat on the go. If almonds aren't your thing, though, try other nutrient-rich nuts such as pistachios, peanuts, pecans, or cashews.

Cold Pasta

I'm going to say it: leftover pasta is best cold—that is, as long as no meat is involved. Pack up your leftover noodles and add a splash of olive oil to enjoy on your outing.

Quinoa Salad

If you're looking for more of a nutritious meal as opposed to a snack, consider a quinoa salad. All you need is a simple dressing, some seasonal vegetables, and a batch of quinoa to make it. For a light dressing, mix together olive oil, salt, pepper, a squirt of lemon juice, a couple of spoonfuls of vinegar, and something sweet such as honey. For the vegetables, look for anything seasonal: peas during the spring, tomatoes during the summer, carrots during the fall, and shallots during the winter.

Flaneuring at Work

I once spent an entire workday only getting up twice: the first time was to use the restroom and the other time to grab lunch. I'm borderline embarrassed to tell you that, reader, but so many of us have experienced this issue given today's unhealthy work-life balance. Unless you live in Scandinavia. (If it weren't so hard to become a citizen, I'd join you life-loving heroes.)

The TL;DR version of this entire chapter is that flaneuring can help you reinvigorate your workday, help kick stress to the curb, and pull you out of the creativity sinkhole you might often find yourself diving into headfirst. We need to get up more often, and we need to be nicer to our brains. Make the true flaneurs—you know, the ones who quietly go about their business romanticizing the world and fully accepting that women can and should do the same—proud of your efforts.

How to Flaneur without Leaving Your Desk

I get it: taking a walk every day just isn't an option for everyone, and I feel that right in the center of my soul. During the workweek, I'm generally going from meeting to meeting or am stuck at my desk answering never-ending emails. My work-life balance grievances are friends with your work-life balance grievances. But you can get some of the benefits of flaneuring without actually going outside.

Go on a Mental Google Earth Vacation

Stick with me here; this is a thing. I cannot count the number of stressful moments that have been smashed after ten minutes of exploring, say, the south coast of Iceland on Google Earth. If you have a moment to get away from your desk, find a quiet place in your office, put on a favorite playlist on your headphones, bring your computer or phone, and pull up Google Earth. Lose yourself in the terrain and street scenes of a different world. Even if it's just for a few moments, it may help ease your stress and lighten the weight of reality.

Stretch It Out

Moving your body is important for a lot of reasons, but it can also help you keep your head on straight. If you can't escape your workload, take one minute to do some stretching. One of my favorite stretches is also one of the most embarrassing to see someone do (if that doesn't say something about my personality, I don't know what does). Position yourself in a deep squat. Make sure your legs are a little more than hip-width apart with a slight angle to your feet (align your toes so they're pointing the same way your knees are). From there, make it more awkward and put your hands in a prayer grasp between your legs and drive your elbows into the insides of your knees. You should feel the stretch deep in your hip adductors. You should also look as if you're taking a camping-style bathroom break. Once you're fully stretched in the legs, stand up and reach your arms as far above your head as possible. Arch your back, take a deep breath, and slowly lower your arms to your sides. Consider this the first step in just feeling better, a task you can continue into your workday flaneuring. While you're going through these steps, do not think about a thing. You can handle that for a few seconds of stretching. Give your brain the simple task of feeling: Take account of how it feels to stretch your body, release any tension you've got building up right out of the tips of your fingers, and breathe. Do not forget to breathe.

Try Being a Cyberflaneur

If you've ever found yourself in a deep hole of Chrome tabs highlighting the various outfits Meghan Markle has worn in the past four years, you've practiced cyber-flaneuring. The idea is the same as physical flaneuring: go where your brain takes you, don't question it, and take careful note of your environment. If you can't leave your desk for an actual walk, take to the Internet. Start with one topic—say, bonsai—and click on whatever piques your interest. Don't worry about whether your click hole makes sense; just let it happen.

If you've done it right, you'll find a wonderful mix of topics at the end of your cyber adventure. On a recent cyberflaneuring session, I found myself with these tabs after fifteen minutes of exploring: a quick-start guide to crocheting, a list of waterfalls to visit in Iceland, a gallery of cute Samoyed photos, a spoiler article on the most recent season of the *Chilling Adventures of Sabrina*, and a list of Airbnbs for Des Moines. What a wonderfully specific look into my life.

One thing to keep in mind: time. Give yourself a set break since, you know, the Internet never ends and it's way too easy to get caught up in YouTube videos of people tripping or dogs bouncing on trampolines.

Take a Lap

OK, technically this requires you to leave your desk . . . but you don't have to leave your office. Keeping a water bottle at my desk may be the best thing I've ever done for my hydration and mental health at work. Think of it this way: If things get tense or overwhelming, you always have an excuse to walk away. Fill up your water bottle. Even if it means chugging half of that bottle before you can add more, you always have a reason to walk away. Take the long way to the water fountain.

During that time, promise me you won't think about work. Even better: think about nothing. You deserve a break.

How Flaneuring Can Help You Handle Stress Better

Studies such as an April 2019 report in *Frontiers in Psychology*[*] by a group of professors at the University of Michigan show that taking a walk will make your life better. Specifically, this study found that taking at least twenty minutes to get out and stroll outside can reduce your stress levels. The study gave this effect a name: the nature pill. The study asked a group of participants to take a ten-minute walk at least three times a week. To measure the success or failure of the walks and their impact on stress levels, each participant was given a

---

[*] M. R. Hunter, B. W. Gillespie, and S. YP. Chen, "Urban Nature Experiences Reduce Stress in the Context of Daily Life Based on Salivary Biomarkers," *Frontiers in Psychology,* April 4, 2019.

saliva swab, which was tested for a change in cortisol, a steroid responsible for hormonal stress reactions. The results showed cortisol levels were 10 percent lower on average after the walks.

During the walks, the participants weren't allowed to talk on the phone, read, hold a conversation, or use social media. It was the purest form of flaneuring. The only requirements were that the walk had to take place during the day and in a place that the walker considered "connecting with nature."

If you can find a forested area in which to flaneur, you're going to be even better off. *Environmental Health and Preventive Medicine* published a study[*] in January 2010 breaking down the physiological benefits of forest bathing. For the uninitiated, forest bathing is simple: get to an area where you're surrounded by nature—ideally,

---

[*] B. J. Park, Y. Tsunetsugu, T. Kasetani, T. Kagawa, and Y. Miyazaki, "The Physiological Effects of *Shinrin-Yoku* (Taking in the Forest Atmosphere or Forest Bathing): Evidence from Field Experiments in 24 Forests across Japan," *Environmental Health and Preventive Medicine*, January 2010.

trees—and take in the atmosphere. Anyway, back to the research: twelve participants took a walk across twenty-four different forests in Japan. On the first day of the experiment, half of the walkers were sent to the forest and the other half to the city. The next day, each group was sent to the location they hadn't yet visited. After each walk, blood pressure, heart rate, pulse rate, and salivary cortisol were measured. I'll bet you can guess the results . . . you already know the forest bathers were calmer and less stressed than the other group.

That said, many of us don't need data to tell us that a little bit of adventure, fresh air, and romanticism is good for the brain. When you realize that work is not the only definition of who you are as a person, you're not only going to feel better, but you'll do your job better.

I work in the magazine industry, a world where advertising sales inform editorial decisions and an incorrect date in a newsletter gives a sponsor control over our next newsletter. I lose my breath at least five times a day, and it's not from running up and down the stairs to and from an afternoon of back-to-back meetings. I don't tell you this to make you question my sanity or feel bad for me; I tell you this because I freak out (internally) a lot. In a moment when the whole world seems to revolve around a typo in a Facebook post, observing a balloon tied to a streetlamp perfectly align with the sun can be therapeutic for me. So when you're dealing with a particularly stressful situation at work, try to either physically or mentally step away from it for a moment, tap into your inner flaneur, and find something beautifully boring to notice.

If this still seems like an impossible task—and give yourself the space and the love to accept that it's totally OK for stepping away to seem futile—focus on your breathing. When I'm walking and get caught up in a particularly stressful thought cycle, or if I just get too winded from trying to catch up with the cute dog in front of me, I occasionally find myself practicing a breathing technique my trainer taught me. Breathe in deep through your nose, then breathe out as if you're pushing air through a straw. This will help you control your diaphragm, which brings you back to reality.

How Flaneuring Can Spark Creativity

Flaneuring is about taking the mind-set of a romantic and applying that to everything you do in a given experience. For example, consider the way early flaneurs regarded maps. Instead of accepting them as they were and giving in to the constraints of a printed border on a piece of paper, they quite literally tore them apart. The original flaneurs were known for cutting up maps and putting them back together. Let's revisit pod-play creator Matt Sosin: he was drawn into the world of flaneuring after discovering how these romantic pioneers regarded the most basic tool of spatial awareness.

"Get a real map and draw a diagonal line through it, and try to follow that line through it as best you can," he shared with me. "[Flaneurs] would take a glass and tape it down, drawing a circle around the rim of the glass, and [then try] to follow that line as best they could around the city."

You might be saying to yourself, "That's cool and all, but how do I get to the creativity level of cutting up a map and completely rewriting the rules of navigating space?" Baby steps, my new friend. Give yourself a moment to remember the lesson behind cutting up those maps: it gives you some direction and will help you take that baby step toward inspiring your own routes. It can spark some major creativity, if you let it. "If you're told to just go, even if you're trying to be very meditative and wander, you're going to have certain proclivities about where you're going to move, even if it's unconscious," Sosin said. "This strips that away from you and makes it more random and chaotic . . . and fun."

Bring this same thought into your own flaneuring sessions at the office. Start small: stare out the window. If you need a prompt, something that brings you out of the here and now, try this: Spend five minutes journaling as if you're visiting for the first time whatever scene lies outside the window. Describe what it looks like, the sounds, the smell, the hike it took to get there. Get romantic about a place you've yet to experience. It'll help you reset your brain and—one hopes—tackle in a more creative and productive manner whatever work project you were stuck on.

Flaneuring as Meditation

In addition to being a wonderful way to destress and ignite creativity, flaneuring can double as a means of practicing mindfulness meditation. According to Laura Teusink, a two-hundred-hour-certified teacher for both yoga and meditation with an inspiring ability to put the feelings associated with meditation into words and teachings, flaneuring shares many similar qualities to a type of meditation called aimless wandering.

"You would think [aimless wandering] were easy, but it's not," Teusink said to me. "We're so used to having an agenda, and we're so used to our minds being in charge. Aimless wandering requires that you put the mind in the back seat and follow other currents of your interior landscape; not just the current of the mind." But don't let that discourage you. (If you need a quick motivational boost or some solid guidance, head back to the "getting started" tips in the beginning of the book.) As we chatted further, Teusink brought up three other things that are often overlooked when practicing aimless wandering: sound, scent, and touch. "You could say I'm going to go aimlessly wander and let the first thing that draws me somewhere be my eyes. Survey the landscape with equanimity first, try not to be attracted to or averse to anything at all, and see what draws your attention," she said. Once you've got that down, choose another sense. "If I follow my nose, where do I go? You could decide aurally, what am I drawn to sound-wise? You could also go with your feeling. If there's a breeze, do I want to walk into it? Do I feel like walking into it or do I want to avoid it?"

When you're flaneuring, you can do the same by taking note of all your senses—not just what you're seeing. Allow yourself to become overwhelmed with how you physically feel: What do you smell? How does your skin feel? What can you hear? Address each thing, filter it, become content with it. Then move on.

How to Meditate and Calm Your Mind Without Making It a Chore

If the idea of meditation brings images of tranquil white-walled rooms with a group of people sitting on round pillows partaking in a deep chorus of *om*s, you're not entirely wrong—but you're also not getting the whole picture, as you can probably guess from what we discussed just a few lines above. Reminder: like flaneuring, meditation can take many forms. While that's a freeing and beautiful thought, it can, too, be intimidating.

But I'm here to tell you that you can meditate while doing a number of flaneuring activities: taking a walk, driving, riding a bike . . . the list goes on and on and on. Thich Nhat Hanh provides an incredible resource for practicing mindful meditation during your mundane tasks. His message is that you can turn any moment into a productive practice for your brain. I was first introduced to his writings in my freshman year at Drake University, when my seminar professor assigned us to read Hanh's book *Peace Is Every Step: The Path of Mindfulness in Everyday Life.* The thin book is easy to miss on a bookshelf, but it's the book that has brought the most into my life. It brought me even more insight than Marie Kondo's *The Life-Changing Magic of Tidying Up,* and that's saying something if you've peeked into my closet anytime recently. Thich Nhat Hanh can teach you how to practice mindfulness while doing the dishes. He can share the secrets of slowing down and catching up with yourself internally while waiting at a stoplight. And, yes, he has thoughts on mindfully walking outside. Once you're done reading *Flâneuse*, I encourage you to grab a copy of *Peace Is Every Step*.

Walk with Me is a documentary about Hanh's monastic lifestyle and the importance he's placed upon walking meditation. In my conversation with Teusink, she shared her own experience being in a space Hanh personally impacted. While describing a time she spent at Blue Cliff Monastery in Pine Bush, New York, she recalled aimlessly wandering the grounds. Visitors were instructed that every time a gong was sounded, they were to stop wherever they were and put on hold any conversation and simply take in their surroundings. You'll see this happen in *Walk with Me*. It takes only a simple action to bring you back to the physical world.

Practicing meditation daily can be an intimidating thought, but there are plenty of ways to start. I reached out to Ellie Burrows, the cofounder of MNDFL, a NYC-based set of studios offering meditation classes to the stressed and overworked masses—or to any looking to center themselves. "MNDFL exists to enable humans to feel good, and we do that by helping them build and/or maintain a meditation practice," Burrows shared with me. "We make meditation accessible and feature expert teachers from a variety of traditions offering simple techniques in an accessible manner. Even if you think you can't meditate, we have teachers who will prove you delightfully wrong. I think we can all agree that New York City is in desperate need of quiet and relaxing spaces. If I was struggling with my practice, and stress levels, in this city, I felt others were probably struggling, too."

Burrows, a former film executive, cofounded the company with Lodro Rinzler, author of *The Buddha Walks into a Bar*. The classes are often themed, some around calming the body down for the night and others for addressing lingering emotions and channeling them into productive meditations.

I reached out to Burrows for a few tips on clearing your mind and quickly learned that clearing your mind isn't necessarily the goal. Rather, it's to intentionally focus on changing the relationship you have to your own internal commentary. "People really like to hold on to the misconception that meditation will 'clear your mind' and teach you how to 'stop thinking,'" Burrows said. "Meditation isn't meant to turn off your mind. In fact, it's a dynamic practice that requires the use of the mind to begin with: it is the act of bringing your mind to an object like the breath or a mantra. One of my first teachers, Emily Fletcher, likes to say, 'The mind involuntarily thinks like the heart involuntarily beats. If we stopped thinking. we'd be dead.'" If you've tried meditation and found yourself unable to reset your thoughts, here's some comfort: "If your expectation is to have zero thoughts during meditation, then you are setting yourself up for disappointment," Burrows says. "I've never had a thoughtless meditation in my life. Sure, meditation can help us change our relationship to our thoughts, but it can't make them disappear."

The best way to become better at slipping into a meditation is by starting slow and running through the following steps while you're comfortably seated somewhere. Burrows uses the workplace as an example of where you can get started—especially because, as we know, work can be particularly stressful—but you can do these steps wherever you are.

1. Find the right place. "If your desk is too distracting or you work at a shared desk, then it could be helpful to identify a space in the office in which you are comfortable practicing. Once you find your special at-work meditation spot, make sure there is a chair or couch. Most offices don't have meditation cushions handy, but that's probably going to change in the near future."

2. Get your position nailed down. "Begin by feeling your sitz bones on the surface you are sitting on, and make sure your feet are firmly planted on the ground about hips' width apart. You can bend your elbows at a ninety-degree angle and then let your hands fall and rest a few

inches from your knees. Your spine should follow its natural curvature and be uplifted. You can tuck your chin in slightly and then relax all the muscles in your face one by one—forehead and cheeks—and then allow your jaw to hang open ever so slightly."

3. Focus on your gaze, but don't get caught up in where you're looking. "If you are practicing eyes open, feel free to set your gaze three to four feet in front of you. Your gaze should be soft and not focused on anything in particular. You can also practice eyes closed as well."

4. Pay attention to your breathing. "Bring your attention to where the breath feels most prominent to you; you don't have to make the breath effortful, change or alter it in any way. Bring your attention to where you feel the breath most easily and naturally; it could be the subtle rise and fall of the chest or the belly, or the soft air that passes in and out of the nostrils. Alternatively, you can

also follow the cycle of the breath, bringing your attention to the inhale, the exhale, and the space in between."

5. Schedule your meditations. "It could also be helpful to schedule your meditations into your workday, so you see them on your calendar just like you would any other commitment, whether personal or professional. Prioritizing the practice can be difficult at first, but once you commit and become consistent, the benefits, which are cumulative over time, will begin to present themselves. And, quite frankly, experiencing those benefits firsthand is the best incentive to keep practicing."

Once you've become more comfortable doing this sitting down, try bringing Burrows's tips for focusing on your breath and scheduling meditations into your day to your flaneuring. If you decide to do this while flaneuring, know that not every walk you take needs to be a meditation—simply try doing it every now and then. If you're looking for another suggestion, Teusink offered up a strategy for acknowledging, addressing, and letting go of fleeting thoughts: physically stop walking. "If you notice yourself getting lost in a thought while you're out on your walk, you could make a rule for yourself: each time you notice your thinking, you stop and take a breath and continue your journey," Teusink says. "If you're stopping, you're really paying attention. That's a way of using the actual act of wandering to support mindfulness. Walk with the goal of perceiving what's coming into your consciousness without judgment and see how far you get before your mind disengages from your immediate surroundings."

While flaneuring should not be overly complicated, remember that it's a time to give your brain a break from the daily grind and intentionally put yourself out there to simply experience and observe. That said, you can most certainly practice meditation while flaneuring. Doing so will get you on the path to a less stressed and happier daily routine. If you've ever thought that you couldn't possibly have enough time in the day to both meditate and wander, I'm here to inform you that you are very, very wrong. But I still like you.

Flaneuring in the World

Flaneurs aren't limited to living in France, you know. I hope you've understood at least that much, given you're this far in the book. People around the world have been wandering with intention for a long time. You might be surprised to learn just how many countries have their own take on the practice. Moreover, you may not realize that many of these global flaneurs have created spaces that take the craft into account in their design. Today, flaneuring has become easier than ever due to the many pop-up experiences that are designed with exploration in mind.

In this chapter, I'll break down some of the ways flaneurs around the world explore their spaces, and some of the spaces that are designed to make flaneurs out of everyone. By understanding the myriad ways you and other humans can flaneur around the globe, you may just open yourself up to a whole world of new cultures to learn about and experiences to have.

Organized Chaos: How Flaneuring Influences Design

Creating a space that helps people get a little lost while also experiencing a specific set of tasks is hard. I mean, just reading that sentence is tough on the brain. All of the following places fall under this category, though, and while they are very different from one another, they all have the shared goal of creating a space meant to be wandered through. Being able to do this kind of wandering—in an environment where someone else has already done all of the potential path-planning—also adds a layer of safety that allows visitors to shed inhibitions. Something is cool about paying some money to put yourself in a world you recognize as "spontaneous to you," which could make your wandering both a little more comfortable and a lot more interesting.

Sleep No More

Housed in the McKittrick Hotel, New York City's *Sleep No More* is an interactive play based on Shakespeare's *Macbeth* that takes visitors through a night of unique experiences. Because of the way the play space is set up, each guest's encounter with the actors will be a bit different from other guests' encounters—meaning some guests could be led into one room, while another group of guests head into a different room, while still other guests become characters in the performance. Guests are also encouraged to explore and volunteer when asked.

Essentially, *Sleep No More* is an entirely contained performance that has one outcome, but still manages to give each guest a different set of memories. That sentence describes what flaneuring is at its core. No one can have the same unique stroll that you did. Getting a play—a manufactured experience—to achieve this same thing? That's not easy. And *Sleep No More* isn't the only place doing this kind of thing.

Meow Wolf

The easiest way to describe Meow Wolf is a Chuck E. Cheese for adults, minus the animatronic animals and sticky counters where you collect your overpriced prizes. It's a giant playhouse and an interactive art installation. Each room is intended to stretch your handle on reality, sometimes calling for you to crawl through a dryer and other times presenting you with a textured wall impossible not to touch.

Located in Santa Fe, New Mexico, the immersive

experience is becoming a chain of sorts—a new location is to open in Las Vegas in 2019, and another is coming to Denver in 2020—partly because it's been made popular by Instagram, so you're bound to get at least a few people blocking your way for the perfect photo. But remember, this place is all about exploration. Step into a new room and find a riddle to solve.

You can also use audio tours to elevate your experience. These tours walk you through the various exhibits and installations, including who's behind them and why they're special to the Meow Wolf experience. Take it a step further with the Anomaly Tracker, an added experience from the creators that tasks visitors with solving a mystery that took place in the house. Using an app, users just need to point their smartphone at the various targets to unlock special activations. Innovations such as this have turned basic Victorian fun houses into the kind of things dreams are made of.

Disney Parks

No matter which Disney park you're visiting, it's impossible to ignore the detail that goes into the guest experience. From the wooden signs calling out all of the various directions to popular rides or experiences to the daily opening of the gate at Magic Kingdom that makes you feel as if you're in an actual dream, there isn't a whole lot of room for uninformed wandering. With so many children passing through the parks every day, I'm sure visibility is high on Disney's list of design elements. But that doesn't mean you can't go on a little hidden adventure within the parks. Ghost Post, a limited-release subscription service launched in 2016, was for Disney fans who wanted to see a new side to the Haunted Mansion ride.

The first 999 people who signed up for Ghost Post received three packages over three months. Each contained a set of items, supposedly from the mansion itself, unlocking part of a mystery surrounding the ride's world. Families with the membership were then encouraged to activate and interact with the items via Disney's Phantom Radio app on their smartphones to help uncover the mystery. Sure, purists may not call this flaneuring given that you're following a set of clues, but I would argue that since you don't know the outcome, this was a great example of a fun way to flaneur with the family.

The Jejune Institute

"To those dark horses with the spirit to look up and see . . . a recondite family awaits."

That's the tagline you'll find if you google *Jejune Institute*. Located in San Francisco, this institute isn't a school, but an unusually immersive game. The backbone of the project, which was led by artist Jeff Hull, was human curiosity—finding a world existing and thriving right in plain sight. Well, that, and the intrigue of an exclusive invitation.

You have to remember that, today, everyone knows this is an alternate-reality game. But when it was first introduced in 2008 as a secret society of sorts, the intent wasn't as clear. Members soon came to know Jejune also as the Institute for the Development of Enhanced Perceptual Awareness, an intriguing title that pulls at our human drive to become better, more aware people. The game unspooled as a series of tasks and steps that required you to head to an office building to inquire about a key, attend protests, and purchase seemingly senseless objects from oddly specific locations. This wild-goose chase involved all of the props you'd imagine it would: typed-out letters, unexpected phone calls from strangers, maps, and mundane objects handpicked with senselessness found in shops around San Francisco, eliciting internal questions such as "What is this institute and why did they just have me pick up a boom box from this store?"

The Jejune Institute has since been revealed as an incredibly elaborate game, meant to pique curiosity and spontaneity. That it did. It makes you wonder just how much is happening around you that you don't know about.

Central Park

Even if you've never been to Central Park, the words spark an image in your mind: massive fields of grass and the Strawberry Fields John Lennon memorial everyone talks about. If you have been, think about what your first impressions of the park were without having been there, then think about your postvisit thoughts. If you pick one path of the park to stick to, you'll walk through tunnels, past baseball fields, along castle ruins (if you're lucky), and right by areas accented by massive rocks encouraging you to stray and do a bit of climbing. Simply put, Central Park is a flaneur's paradise.

The design of the park encourages spontaneous adventure. The numerous benches aren't a mistake: they're placed to encourage loitering. Pay attention to them and you'll notice they climb around areas designated for watching *something*, whether it's a baseball game, runners making their way around the reservoir, or the people visiting the Central Park Zoo. This ideology expands into parks all around the world.

You don't need to have known the designers of Central Park—Frederick Law Olmsted and Calvert Vaux—to understand what they were getting at. The aforementioned boulders are a great example: Every so often, you'll notice stacks of giant rocks lining a walking path. They're big enough to climb, but not so big that they scare anyone off. These serve as alternative seating options, places to recline where there are no benches or the benches are full of butts. Pay a visit to Brooklyn to check out Prospect Park, another design from the architect duo. Turn it into your own flaneuring game to try to spot the similarities in the park styles.

Cruise Ships

As with Central Park, it doesn't take too much imagination to think of all the activities you can partake in on a cruise ship. Indulge me as I, a person who has never been on a cruise, list them: eat, swim, sleep, shop, gamble, sing karaoke, join a trivia team, go to the spa, take a walk, go to a yoga class, lift weights, take a cooking class, watch a movie, see a play, listen to live music, eat again. I've confirmed this list to be accurate—and unedited!—by friends who have been on cruises. I repeat: you can do all of these things on a cruise ship.

These massive boats may have set itineraries, but the people on them don't necessarily. The days spent in between land excursions were made for wandering. You're encouraged to explore, and no single pamphlet could share all of the different activities available to cruisers. If you don't mind wandering alongside thousands of other strangers, then this could be considered the ultimate flaneur's vacation . . . but maybe just for extroverted flaneurs.

Flaneurs around the Globe

As I mentioned earlier, romanticism is far from unique to one area of the world—every country has its own take on flaneuring or intentional wandering, whether it be while catching up with a friend, exploring nature as a child, or simply being French. Here are just a few of the flaneuring methods of romantics across the world.

The French: The Original Flaneurs

We covered these tired, old nineteenth-century dudes at the beginning of this book, but has flaneuring kept its hold on French society? The answer is a resounding yes, but you won't necessarily find people talking about it. It's a given that strolling is just a part of life.

How could it not be when you have so many romantic, picturesque cities surrounding you?

Anne Berest, Audrey Diwan, Caroline de Maigret, and Sophie Mas described it best in a chapter of their book *How to Be Parisian Wherever You Are*: "A Parisienne always has a good reason to be sitting on a bench." In the book, there's a particular illustration of the many reasons a Frenchwoman may find herself out on said bench. My favorite reason is "When she is walking out for a good reason and slams the door behind her to show she means business, and then realises she has no idea where to go." Follow that up with another statement from a few paragraphs down and you'll have a good grip on an important aspect of the French culture: "When she wants to imagine what it will be like to be an old woman in Paris one day, talking to the pigeons for lack of better company." This is a valid reminder that an empty bench is full of opportunities and is always there for you when you need it most, whether you need a space to dream up the future or catch your breath.

Ugandan Friendship Walks

When two male friends go for a walk in Uganda, whether it be down the main street or to the end of a driveway, they hold hands. I spent a month during the summer in between my sophomore and junior years of college studying in Kampala, the capital of Uganda. It was a strange time—given that the popularity of the Old Testament could, at times, create a hostile environment for the LGBTQ+ community members living in the country—and I became intrigued by this wonderful show of affection between two members of the same sex in a place you (unfortunately) wouldn't associate with such a scene. From my new friend Moses, a Ugandan university student from the local group of students who spent time with us for that month, I found out that this was a common cultural act. When two friends want to catch up, they take a walk and hold hands. They share details from their days, discuss current events, and gossip about their friends. Where they walk isn't important; the conversations they have are the whole point.

This kind of flaneuring is less about observing your surroundings. Rather, it's about finding the significance in the words of a loved one while you wander.

United Kingdom's Right to Roam

You might remember the UK roamers I spoke about in the section "A Somewhat Long Note on the Importance of Romanticism" earlier in the book. Well, a fun little law in the United Kingdom called the Right to Roam applies to these people. The United Kingdom is home to more distance walkers than you can count, and for good reason: trespassing isn't necessarily illegal. While still a punishable crime for those attempting to harm or wreak havoc, trespassing is generally a pretty trivial thing. The *99% Invisible* podcast—which mainly focuses on design and architecture, with the occasional branch-off—did a great episode that talks about this law and some of the people who appreciate it. For instance, one of the podcast's producers, Katie Mingle, shared the story of her father's unknowingly walking onto Madonna's private property. Instead of a fine or an arrest, he was treated to a lovely conversation with a member of Madonna's staff after hitchhiking a ride back to where he was staying. Something beautiful and romantic is in that kind of innocent ignorance. It's episode 313, if you're interested in hearing more about it.

A quick note for the love of safety and all that is good in life: Please don't knowingly trespass if you're not in the United Kingdom or a country that practices right to roam. The tired and not-so-funny trope of being run off a property by a landowner with a gun in hand is overused for a reason. Do yourself a big, potentially lifesaving favor: start with a public property. And the kinds of activities you can freely participate in on access land are limited. According to the "Right to Roam" section on the United Kingdom's official website, to avoid a fine steer clear of "horse-riding, cycling, camping, taking animals other than dogs on to the land, driving a vehicle (except mobility scooters and powered wheelchairs), and water sports."

A group called the Ramblers based in the United Kingdom are focused on maintaining and raising awareness around public paths. A current campaign called "Don't Lose Your Way" is aimed at creating a map of the 140,000 miles of public pathways that cross England and Wales. The Ramblers website shares that some of these walkways date back to medieval times, connecting various settlements and villages. If these paths aren't put on an official map before January 1, 2026, they could lose funding for preserving and maintaining them for generations to come. Just imagine if every other country on earth put this kind of emphasis on maintaining public walkways.

The Nordic Countries' Connection to Nature

Growing up in the Nordic countries—Denmark, Iceland, Finland, Sweden, and Norway—is about as different from growing up in, say, Milwaukee as a tomato and an avocado are different in color. (That was not a surprising sentence.) In Scandinavia, you'll find childhood often takes place outside—and it's about more than getting some fresh air. Think of it as connecting with the plants and natural environments as an intimate part of life, not simply an item on a checklist that leads to a healthy upbringing. Children often head out after breakfast during the summer and do not return until dinnertime. I've met people in Iceland who have laughed at my simultaneous shock and concern when they tell me this, usually followed by some kind of polite criticism of the lack of green space in New York City. Despite the intense natural danger in a country where two tectonic plates meet, parents let their children roam outside during the light of day (and into the night, given the summer's midnight sun).

Don't mistake this for negligence—so many of Nordic countries top the list of Happiest Places on Earth for a reason. This kind of freedom, to experience the springtime blooms without someone telling you they're beautiful, is taught early on, not from a lesson book or in-class video, but from pure discovery. The Nordic countries' emphasis on connecting to nature at an early age has fostered generations of flaneurs.

The Italian Passeggiata

Much like the word *flaneur*, *passeggiata* is not as intimidating as it sounds. If you've ever taken a postdinner stroll—or a walk after aggressively snacking—then you've partaken in this quintessential Italian pastime. *Passeggiata* is the ritual of taking a walk after dinner. Not only is it intended to help kick-start digestion, but it's also become a social activity, a moment to catch up with dinner dates. Italy's incredibly romantic architecture would be the exact motivation I would need to crawl out of the couch after a meal.

One trip to Italy and you can see the way communities have built public spaces for this ritual. Public squares buzz late into the night with teenagers taking seemingly innocent walks with their crushes, older friends enjoying a glass of wine at a café along the edge of the square, and others just walking alone to show off a fashionable outfit.

The nightly *passeggiata* is seen as an opportunity to flaunt your best style. Locals dress up and, as they pass, gossip on what (or who) everyone is wearing. If you're visiting the country, have a bit of fun and pack an outfit you've deemed too fancy or fussy for everyday life. There's no time like *passeggiata* time in Italy to make a bit of a scene.

You'll find the main street or square of every city in Italy busiest between 5:00 p.m. and 8:00 p.m., with a few early birds and stragglers passing through before and after. Summer makes for the best strolling, with locals partaking nearly every day in the south of the country. If you're lucky, someone might even invite you on a special *passeggiata* to a nearby beach.

Australian Walkabouts

The ritualistic stroll so important to the culture of aboriginal Australians comes with a good dose of intent. This hike across indigenous land is integral to the coming of age of young men in the culture. It's considered a rite of passage and represents their spiritual transition into adulthood. That said, at its core, I would consider a person on a walkabout to be a flaneur.

There's no telling how long a walkabout will last; it could be twelve days or six months before a young man makes it home again. The elders of an aboriginal community decide when each boy is ready to go on the journey (talk about abandoning all control), and the experience is focused on survival, being able to overcome the environment, and adaptation. If that's not flaneuring at its most intense—especially given some of the incredibly dangerous wildlife on the continent—I would love to know what is.

German Geocaching

First, let's define *geocaching*. An in-depth study by Daniel Telaar, Antonio Krüger, and Johannes Schöning of the University of Münster, the German Research Center for Artificial Intelligence, and Hasselt University, respectively, titled "A Large-Scale Quantitative Survey of the German Geocaching Community in 2007,"[*] says it both succinctly and in proper detail in this quote:

- It's a location-based experience that has established and sustained itself over several years (starting in 2000).

---

[*] D. Telaar, A. Krüger, and J. Schöning, "A Large-Scale Quantitative Survey of the German Geocaching Community in 2007," *Advances in Human-Computer Interaction* 2014 (June 26, 2014).

- It involves both the consumption and the creation of experiences.

- It is a game that uses extensively virtual and physical representations and involves a mobile device.

Consider these the golden rules of geocaching. Since Germany has the world's largest community of geocachers, you could consider these the golden rules of any interaction you have in Germany. I'll leave that up to you.

If you haven't caught on yet, Germans take geocaching **VERY SERIOUSLY**. If I could make those capital letters as big as a single page, I would. The idea behind geocaching is that special little elements and experiences are hidden in plain sight. The caches are designed to be right underneath your nose—it makes finding one that much more exciting. Some companies in Germany, and beyond, are even focused on creating everyday structures with hidden nooks and crannies perfect for hiding caches (think a pole with a secret chamber that's accessed by finding a barely visible seam).

You might think, "Hey, since they aren't looking for something specific, this can't possibly fall into the magical world of flaneuring." I would argue that you, my friend, are wrong. Flaneuring was originally an outlet for drunken men to romanticize the mundane (we've been over that). Trying to uncover a secret that is quite possibly waiting for you inside a hidden compartment in a tree stump? If that's not adding infinite possibility to an inanimate object you would simply walk by any other day, then I'll give in and tell my mother that she's right the next time she tries to tell me Claritin will "fix" my sinus infection. And I refuse to do that, so that means I've got to be right.

Geocaching is more related to traditional flaneuring than you would think. According to Telaar, Krüger, and Schöning's work, one finds a geocache only after solving a problem. Think of it as like the original flaneurs cutting up maps and attempting to create a new way of looking at a space. Geocachers often put themselves through a series of brain teasers and riddles before figuring out their right direction. Just imagine a bunch of older French dudes (top hats, eyeglasses, shiny shoes) equipped with a GPS and logbooks politely knocking against trees and other things in search of a mystery object.

Wandering While Traveling

One of the best ways to experience a new place and the people who live there is by wandering—in the safest way possible. Make sure you know, generally, where you are, where your hotel or Airbnb is, and the parts of town that may be better left to someone familiar with the surroundings. When I first moved to Brooklyn, I explored my new home by hopping on the train every Saturday with a new neighborhood in mind. One weekend it might be Harlem, another it was Chinatown, and the next it was Bay Ridge. Being an intern, I had about $20 I could dedicate to the day's activities, which I more often than not set aside for lunch. I would get off at a train station central to a neighborhood and start walking. I'd pop into stores, smile at people passing by, buy an especially intriguing bouquet of flowers just for fun, or maybe grab a drink from a friendly looking bartender. As I got older—and my salary stabilized—the afternoon walks turned into day trips upstate to wander in and out of antique shops and stare at art, should a museum appear.

Being a flaneur is the ultimate way to introduce yourself to a new city, or even your own city. Consider this a guide to stepping into the role with confidence on your next trip (or free weekend).

Where to Start

If you're visiting a new city, or country, and you're staying at a hotel, take advantage of the concierge and their immense local knowledge. Ask about special neighborhoods rather than specific places and things to see. Don't worry so much about the itinerary of the day; that will work itself out. Also make sure to ask about the areas you should avoid. If a hotel stay is not in your cards, head to a busy bar or café and ask the bartender or barista as they're making your drink. This will also help you steer clear of the tourist trail. Though sticking to the hot spots can be fun if you're looking to people-watch.

How to Avoid Itinerary Guilt

I can already feel it. You're trying hard not to say, "But what if I completely mess up, don't see anything, and end up regretting it?" Let's start by lowering the vacation expectation a little bit. If anything, you'll be seeing a more genuine version of your destination when no tour guides or hordes of fellow tourists are involved. And I don't think you should flaneur your way through an entire vacation. That may be appealing for some people, but give yourself some time to see the sights. As a travel writer, I understand the importance of a bucket list.

Be sure to remind yourself that you are certainly not *wasting* time. You're experiencing a new place in a pure way by watching everyone else experiencing said place. Being an observer allows you to take in details you wouldn't have noticed had you joined the masses. The distance between buildings; the speed of a line and its inchworm-like movement; the different smells of flowers in various front yards as you walk between stoplights; the collective sound of a city, from the car noises to the presence (or lack of) birdsong. Brains are great, but you'll pick up on so many things while flaneuring that you wouldn't have noticed had you had a specific itinerary.

Start by dedicating an afternoon early in your trip to walking around. If you love it, find some additional time to do it again. If you hate it, think about the parts you didn't like. Don't write it off immediately; maybe it was the neighborhood or the time of day you went out wandering. Were you hungry and found it hard to calm your mind? Bring a snack next time. Were you too distracted by making sure everyone else you were traveling with was having a good time? Well, stop that, because you're also on vacation. Sometimes it's easier to flaneur with a pen and paper within reach. Not only is it good to write down all of the things you see and experience, it's good to write down the things that are bothering you as well.

Getting Off the Tourist Trail

This is a lot easier than it sounds. Whenever I buy a plane ticket, I'll scour Instagram for local influencers. Once I find a handful with photos of destinations that intrigue me, I'll slide into the DMs to ask about their favorite places to visit there. I've found secluded hot springs in Iceland, an unbelievable distillery in Vail, and the prettiest castle in Portugal from reaching out to influencers. If that's not quite your speed, do a bit of extra research before your trip. Instead of looking for specific sites to see, focus on the best neighborhoods to visit. That ensures that you'll have a good mix of bars, cafés, restaurants, shops, and activities to select from if you find yourself unable to disconnect for a bit.

If you're visiting a big city—think New York, Madrid, Paris, Tokyo, you get the idea—read a book focused on the destination, or better yet a specific neighborhood in that destination, before you go. This will add context and depth to your flaneuring there. It's a beautiful thing to recognize a street name from *A Tree Grows in Brooklyn* as you're walking through Williamsburg.

Connecting with Others through Flaneuring

Sometimes it's not easy to keep a friendship or romantic relationship going strong for years—or from miles and miles away. But what better way to try than by sharing treasured moments of quiet time? From starting and committing to a creative project that spans years to keeping a regular observation diary you only share with someone you care about, flaneuring offers all kinds of ways to feel connected to others.

Walk with a Buddy

This advice needs no detailed description. Simply call up a friend and plan a couple of hours for some walking. I like to set a destination—say, drinks at a new bar or a movie—but I give my friends and me plenty of time to get to said destination. This way you have something to look forward to and you can give yourself time to take in your surroundings.

Ongoing Personal Projects

Every other Sunday night, my partner, Joseph, spends about two hours chatting with his best friend from college on Google Hangouts. He lives on the West Coast and they haven't seen each other since graduation more than a decade ago, but their friendship is one of the most special ones I've ever been around. (I should also note that I have yet to meet him.) They share photographs they've both taken since they've last spoken and critique each other's work. Both are talented photographers who are especially interested in candid street scenes.

Every two weeks, they share the same prompt: get outside and take photos, with no direction on where or when. Sometimes Joseph will head out in the late afternoon to catch the golden light that takes over lower Manhattan, and other times he'll grab an hour to walk Chinatown just before it's too dark to shoot. The two friends, while capturing other people in the middle of running errands, phone calls, conversations, and commutes, are flaneuring in their own way. It's one of the most beautiful methods to connect with a friend separated by miles.

Finding a way to experience life with a loved one separated by an airplane trip or long car ride isn't easy, but taking the time to find your shared activity is so worth it. Joseph and his friend have shared hundreds of photos, and both have grown as photographers—and creatives—thanks to their mutual feedback. For you, maybe it could be committing to a weekly walk down a new street and writing down all of the details you notice to share with someone you love every time you see them (and the same would go for them). Or it could be meeting up with this person when you're both in the same city to have a walking catch-up conversation. Whatever your flaneur love language is, go with it.

Video Games and Apps

Yes, we are going there. Two video games come to mind when I think of how we can be flaneurs in a more digital world: *Minecraft* and *Ingress*. Both games encourage the player to roam either while interacting with other players or alone. This is not traditional flaneuring in any sense of the definition because:

1. You're not physically moving your body.

2. Cheat codes exist and are easily searchable on the Internet.

3. Flaneuring is meant to take out the conscious direction of a journey, and in a video game you're always going to have control over what your avatar is doing.

Take a stroll back to your childhood and think about *Pokémon*. Now fast-forward to that fateful day when Niantic announced it was making a *Pokémon* app for smartphones. I don't know about you, but I spent a little bit of time being annoyed that Android users got the app first . . . and that was forgotten quicker than a Bulbasaur passing through Cerulean City once it became available for iPhone users. Suddenly, walking to meetings got more interesting—who knew if a Bellsprout would reveal itself outside the shared kitchen. Life also got more dangerous: I definitely walked into more people and once had an unfortunate and literal run-in with an outward-swinging door in Midtown. But I digress. . . .

Video games are constantly shifting into our own realities and making it easier to share this progress with our loved ones. What started as a simple survival and building task in *Minecraft* has turned into *Pokémon Go*. And now we have virtual reality. Being able to put on a pair of goggles and experience a castle town in Portugal via video—something the video team put together while I was an editor at *Travel + Leisure*—is incredible. Virtual reality is making it more accessible for us all to stroll around the world and share experiences with others without buying a plane ticket.

It's becoming easier than ever to share a digital experience with someone near or far. Find one that you're both excited about and get into it.

Ingress

Ingress deserves its own callout here. Released in late 2013 for Android and in mid-2014 for iPhone, the app uses current location coordinates to create various real-time portals for players. Exotic Matter, a strange energy, has divided humans into two groups, and the player must choose a side and fight for its collective cause. By visiting physical landmarks and interacting with them with the app, the user gains important information and tools to empower the player's team.

The game is much more nuanced than that, but you get the idea: the game blurs the line between reality and digital experience, while allowing players to communicate with one another from across the world. These connections can also occur in real life as users meet up to play the game together in smaller, local chapters. This satisfies one of the tougher objectives of flaneuring: discovering even more details in what you already thought were the details of a larger scene. With this last note, Ingress ties into our theme of flaneuring with friends. Find a buddy who is especially interested in gaming, sign up together, and check out some of the local meetups. In no time you'll be flaneuring every day and swapping stories about your encounters.

Regular Journal Trades

Being in a long-distance relationship is hard; there is no other way to describe that. When distance makes it impossible for a loved one to share an experience with you, do the next best thing: keep a daily diary (both of you) and trade them when you see each other. Continue the journaling in your partner's diary and keep the pattern going. After a while, you'll have two physical examples of your time apart and a beautiful mix of each other's encounters. Consistency is key here, so set up daily time to jot down your thoughts.

I'll take a tiny moment to bring in my love for all things crafty—which makes up 75 percent of my will to live. Find a photo you love of the two of you and print two miniature copies, small enough to be glued into the inside cover of each journal. Just imagine how tickled you'll be seventy years (or more) down the road when you find a journal *and* a photo of the age you were when you were swapping daily observations. You're welcome.

Flaneur for a Better Life

Whether you're looking for a new experience, a place to escape to where you can blend into the background, a way to catch up with a friend who loves walking as much as you do, or simply a better, more interesting life—flaneuring is for you. This isn't the nineteenth century, so go out and own those paths, roads, streets, farmers' markets, and local supercenters. Doing so will make you more observant, creative, and mindful—and I hope give you a better quality of life. At the very least, flaneuring will help you become more aware of how horrible others are at sharing the sidewalk. (Never be the person who doesn't share the sidewalk.)

We know that walking outside can lower your physical stress. It can also be a welcome respite when you're feeling overwhelmed at work. Stepping outside your office can have immediate effects on your blood pressure and decision making. Since science says it'll lower your blood pressure, you know what you've got to do: make scientists happy and take a walk outside at least once a day.

As we age gracefully and gratefully (we're all doing that, right?), the physical activity of strolling will set up our bones for success as we get older. The more years you have under your belt, the harder it will be to go on long walks. But we all have our limits no matter how old we are, so there's no excuse to not start flaneuring. Just going outside and taking a stroll for a few minutes to observe your surroundings will help take your stress levels down a few notches and clear your mind. If walking is not the most accessible activity for you, start by walking up and down your driveway or taking a drive. If walking is completely out of the question, you can start flaneuring simply by being outside and taking in the sights and the fresh air. Let your mind wander and take in the scene from where you're sitting. Flaneuring is for all people, even those who aren't physically moving.

Last, but certainly not least, the ability to give more meaning to the mundane parts of your daily life is an extraordinary skill. Not only will this help your unconscious self become more creative and detailed in what it remembers from your past, but it makes walking around in the world all the more fun.

As a parting gift, I'll leave you with a memory from one of my recent wanders, and to say it brought some joy into my life is a complete understatement—I consider it more a stand-up example of how the power of observation can add a delightful layer to your day. It was a Saturday and an impromptu rainstorm sent me rushing into the subway to get from Brooklyn to Manhattan. While I was walking through the station,

I passed a woman whose jacket perfectly blended into the pasted movie ad behind her on the wall; the bright pink was fluorescent enough to hurt my eyes. The kind of color you remember. And somehow the world seemed to match. At that very moment I was paying attention, this absurdly colored jacket blended in with the scene behind it. The best part? The top of the ad on the wall showed a massive watering can showering the image she was obstructing. To me? This woman was a flower, one that was angrily addressing some app on her phone with a sour look on her face . . . about to be doused in water. It put a smile on my face and a giggle in my throat as the subway doors closed and the train slowly pulled out of the station.

Acknowledgments

A massive thank-you to Lauren Elkin for sharing her beautiful insight and stories, Laura Teusink for being a never-ending fountain of calming tips and life-changing work, Matt Sosin for coming up with the coolest idea and sharing it with me, and Ellie Burrows for breaking down meditation in a way I can finally understand.

Six lifetimes of thank-yous to my editor, Lauren Hummel, for gracefully guiding me through editing this book. I've worked with so many editors and I can honestly say I never broke out in sweats or hives when one of your emails hit my inbox. You are a gem.

Laura D, your love of walking is inspiring—our morning flaneurs are some of my favorite city memories. Thank you for taking the time to be a dear friend . . . and helping me get my writing research done in a fun way.

Mom and Dad, thanks for not thinking I was crazy when I studied magazine journalism—that blind and passionate trust and encouragement gets me through the hardest obstacles (such as writing a book on mindful walking). Everything always works out!

Joseph, thank you for believing in me, always, for reminding me what I'm capable of, and for not judging me when I stress-ate popsicles at the dining room table while writing this. I love you.

Last, it would be impossible to apologize to every single person I physically ran my body into on the Brooklyn Bridge while becoming a better flaneur. Thank you for your forbearance, dear bruised strangers.